Wikiworld

Wikiworld

JUHA SUORANTA and TERE VADÉN

PlutoPress
www.plutobooks.com

First published 2010 by Pluto Press
345 Archway Road, London N6 5AA and
175 Fifth Avenue, New York, NY 10010

www.plutobooks.com

Distributed in the United States of America exclusively by
Palgrave Macmillan, a division of St. Martin's Press LLC,
175 Fifth Avenue, New York, NY 10010

British Library Cataloguing in Publication Data
A catalogue record for this book is available from the British Library

ISBN   978 0 7453 2892 8   Hardback
ISBN   978 0 7453 2891 1   Paperback

Library of Congress Cataloging in Publication Data applied for

This book is printed on paper suitable for recycling and made from
fully managed and sustained forest sources. Logging, pulping and
manufacturing processes are expected to conform to the environmental
standards of the country of origin.

10   9   8   7   6   5   4   3   2   1

Designed and produced for Pluto Press by
Chase Publishing Services Ltd, 33 Livonia Road, Sidmouth, EX10 9JB, England
Typeset from disk by Stanford DTP Services, Northampton, England
Printed and bound in the European Union by
CPI Antony Rowe, Chippenham and Eastbourne

*Dedicated to the editors and users of wikis,
wherever you are*

CONTENTS

LIST OF TABLES

ACKNOWLEDGEMENTS

This book includes a part of our joint collaborations, and concludes a research project that has continued for the last six years. We would like to thank the following persons for sharing their ideas on various themes related to the Wikiworld: Michele Knobel, Reijo Kupiainen, Colin Lankshear, Teemu Leinonen, Peter McLaren, Teemu Mikkonen and Niklas Vainio. Our sincere thanks go to the many colleagues and peers on the Net who have discussed our work in progress. We would like to express our heartfelt gratitude to Catherine Preus who corrected and proofread our English, and made many useful comments during the writing and editing process. The editors at Pluto Press, especially Anne Beech, made a courageous decision in publishing the book and helped us tremendously in shaping it into its current form; thank you all!

INTRODUCTION

In the following pages we will argue that the Wikiworld – a set of collaborative practices on the Net as defined below – will advance peoples' autonomy, self-government and actual freedom. The Wikiworld is a system of collective processes rather than a system of ready-made facts given from above, from those who believe that they know better than the rest of us. The Wikiworld is an empowering social construction with positive effects for both political and epistemological democracy and, as we believe, eventually it has the potential to abolish the distinction between the rulers and the ruled. By theorising the basic tenets of the Wikiworld our aim is to advance the world in which this apparently perpetual division is no longer necessary, and can be seen, as Gramsci once said, only as 'a historical fact corresponding to certain conditions' (Gramsci 1971, p. 44). Thus we focus on these 'certain conditions' by claiming that the Wikiworld's central characteristics and practices, those of voluntary participation, sharing and anonymous collectivism, are practices of actual freedom.

Our writing of this book has been driven by several recent promises and possibilities, especially in the area of education and digital media. These include a new ethos of participation, collaboration and co-operation in many branches of activity in the digital sphere; the new openness of academic and other types of publishing is one example. As we argue in this book, we are moving towards a progressive transformation from the institutionalised and individualised forms of learning to open learning and collaboration. This book is born out of the tension between, on one hand, a fascination with the use of new technologies and learning practices in furthering socially just futures, and, on the other hand, a critical view of the constants or 'unmoved movers' (first causes) of the information society development: the West and Capitalism. In short, our task is to explore the promises of open access and the power of critical pedagogy in the context that in this book we call the Wikiworld.

By the notion of Wikiworld we refer to both the technical and the social spheres of the Internet; more specifically to those social formations and political struggles that can be enforced by the possibilities of the Net. The Wikiworld is built through the 'collaborative turn', or what is called participatory culture, which includes relatively low barriers to civic engagement and activism, artistic and other sorts of expression, easy access for creating and sharing one's outputs with others, peer-to-peer relations and informal mentorship, as well as new forms of socialisation, social connections, collectivism and solidarity (see Jenkins et al. 2006). And more than that: from our point of view, the Wikiworld, and its phenomena, is not sufficiently scrutinised if not seen in the larger socio-political context through the lens of radical political economy. From this angle the Wikiworld is also an ideological battlefield, and the stakes are high: in question are the very ways in which we conceive of the digital sphere and its physical counterparts.

A case in point in the collaborative turn is Wikipedia and its sister projects like Wikiversity, which in our estimation will soon confront national educational systems. Researchers, educators, teachers and other cultural workers are tired of waiting to get on board the Wikiworld through their institutions, and are building their blogs and wikis and forming alliances globally with their peers and like-minded people. They are part of informal networks and 'invisible colleges'. Some of them have joined digital temporary autonomous zones. New forms of interaction and knowledge production are flourishing outside closed educational systems. Old organisational structures are like dinosaurs preparing for extinction in the new era. And the potential goes beyond the transformation from formal education to public education: there is Wikinews, Wikileaks, Wikibooks, not to mention all the grass-roots wikis of specific communities. These social inventions are taking research communities back home: to the diverse forms of co-operation free from the pressing and often alienating *modus operandi* of the market universities, national boundaries, and language barriers. Wikipedia and its sister projects have proved the effectiveness of voluntary work in producing and creating free content. These contents have no market value; instead they have huge use value in terms of genuine intellectual interest, unreified sociality and the search for knowledge. The autonomy of science and public education gains from the freedom of the Wikiworld. In terms of education, the Wikiworld comprises some of the key ideas of the Cape Town Open Education Declaration (2008), which is part of a larger global collaborative turn towards open education and open access to knowledge:

> We are on the cusp of a global revolution in teaching and learning. Educators worldwide are developing a vast pool of educational resources on the Internet, open and free for all to use. These educators are creating a world where each and every person on earth can access and contribute to the sum of all human knowledge. They are also planting the seeds of a new pedagogy where educators and learners create, shape and evolve knowledge together, deepening their skills and understanding as they go. This emerging open education movement combines the established tradition of sharing good ideas with fellow educators and the collaborative, interactive culture of the Internet. It is built on the belief that everyone should have the freedom to use, customise, improve and redistribute educational resources without constraint. Educators, learners and others who share this belief are gathering together as part of a worldwide effort to make education both more accessible and more effective. (http://www.capetown-declaration.org/read-the-declaration)

Current international and national trends in educational policies emphasising educational qualifications, competition and marketisation of higher education are too narrow and repressive to last. They distort learning and research just as the notions of 'German' and 'Soviet' science did in their time. In contrast, internationally open and free scientific activity benefits all people and nations equally; otherwise it does not deserve to be called science. But openness is a challenge for closed educational and other systems; it forces educational authorities – public and private alike – to abandon short-sighted monetary aims. Profit-orientation (competition, evaluation, quality control) must be replaced by diversity, conviviality, collaboration, actual freedom, accessibility and participation. Again, this goes beyond the agenda of formal education. As the rallying cry of the Swedish Pirate Party goes, the goal is 'to make the totality of human culture available for everyone'. And not just available: the Wikiworld is also editable, improvable.

By making this book an open access publication we wanted to foster these ideas. This is also a political statement. Since we work in a public university funded by the Finnish government (for how long, we don't know; the publicly funded university system has been in a state of turbulence for years), we are obliged to do our job for the public without cashing in, or without putting some extra cash in our own pockets. Perhaps, if we were independent agents, the case would be different, as we would need to bring bread to the table without a monthly pay cheque from the university. But even that situation shouldn't prevent us from writing and publishing open access; quite the reverse.

Our work is inspired by a definition of the political that can be derived from French philosopher Jacques Rancière: 'Human beings are political, then, because they are literary, because the meanings of words are contested and struggled over in disputes between the powerful and the powerless, those who have to date determined the meaning of words and those who have not' (Hewlett 2007, p. 99).

Open access publishing fits extremely well with the core ideas of critical education as it cherishes collaborative learning in its various forms, and sharing critical ideas and crucial personal and collective experiences. And, as Joe Kincheloe (2007, p. 10), one of the founding figures of critical pedagogy, put it:

> a vibrant, relevant, effective critical pedagogy in the contemporary era must be simultaneously intellectually rigorous and accessible to multiple audiences. In an era when open-access publishing on the Internet is a compelling issue in the politics of knowledge (Willinsky 2006), I contend

that open-access writing and speaking about critical pedagogy are also profoundly important.

This is where the philosophy of open access meets the philosophy of critical education; in the era of corporate rule in the mainstream media (including the academic publishing business), and elsewhere, critical thought and open access need and nourish each other, perhaps more than ever (see, for example, the on-line presence of Paulo Freire at http://freireproject.org).

In a fundamental sense, the social and digital collaborative sphere, the Wikiworld, is anarchistic in its very nature. This means that we cannot channel, control or predict the future of the Wikiworld in advance. But we can offer insights, ideas and collaborative productions which at best can free our minds from the restrictions of the closed system logics. To say that the Wikiworld is anarchistic is not to deny that it is also overdetermined, that is, its development is caused by the multiple actions of the multiple actors. To paraphrase philosopher J. L. Austin (1911–1960), the question on the Wikiworld is not only *How To Do Things with Words*, but also *How To Do Things with Edits, Saves, Uploads, Downloads, Histories, Revisions, and Discussions*.

The book is divided into six chapters. We start the first chapter by locating our position in the critical discussion on education and maintain that there actually is a tradition of educational research and thought that helps in understanding the various characteristics of the Wikiworld. Furthermore, this tradition can be advanced by theorising the tools of the Wikiworld in the context of a critical educational paradigm. In the second chapter, we analyse some of the central, often taken-for-granted assumptions and conceptual schemes of the present age. We adopt the view of political economy in making a division between a netocratic elite and those supposed to be passive consumers. The third chapter deals with the question of radical monopolies, their problems as well as the possibilities of overcoming them with radical openness in the educational and other arenas. In the fourth chapter, we continue with the theme of the present divided world, especially focusing on the youth question and evolving forms of socialisation. The fifth chapter is dedicated to the issue of collaborative learning, particularly in the context of higher education. As the title of our last chapter states, the essential issue in the Wikiworld is one of freedom – levels and kinds of freedom. Our message is clear: we write for the radical openness of education for all.

1

A CRITICAL PARADIGM OF EDUCATION

In his critique of political economy, Marx did not care much about Nature as such, but about how human beings in their social relations use its resources for their own purposes. He was interested in relations between material substratum, capital and labour, which 'is a creator of use value, is useful labour, it is a necessary condition, independent of all forms of society, for the existence of the human race; it is an eternal nature-imposed necessity, without which there can be no material exchanges between man and Nature, and therefore no life' (Marx 1867). Marx put his emphasis on examining how it can be that the coat may be 'worth twice as much as the ten yards of linen'. In the discourse of digital media and digital literacy it is sometimes, perhaps too often, maintained that digitalisation and digital apparatus are master movers that change the world and us by their mere existence. This is partly true if we take it that material being affects human consciousness. But as we see it, more interesting and more important than binary strings of ones and zeros – these rolls of linen of our time – are the uses, and perhaps misuses, of digital media and digital literacy.

Thus digitalisation as such is not the subject of our book, but what we as human beings can make of it. In this sense we tentatively define digital literacies as various processes of using digital information and communication technologies for the common good. In this book, digital literacy refers not only to the ability to use digital technologies – whether personal devices or communication networks – to locate, create and evaluate information, but also and more importantly to build alliances to increase material, social and individual justice and enable social transformation. These aims are shared in the tradition of critical pedagogy and by critical theorists in education who claim that at present we are witnessing and living through the first steps of a true revolution in the modes of digital communication and the creation of convivial tools for collaborative literacy and transformative learning.

> To dramatize the issues at stake, we should consider the claim that we are now undergoing one of the most significant technological revolutions for education since the progression from oral to print and book-based teaching. ... Furthermore, the technological developments of the present era make possible the radical re-visioning and reconstruction of education and society argued for in the progressive era by Dewey and in the 1960s and 1970s by Ivan Illich, Paulo Freire, and others who sought radical educational and social reform. (Kellner 2004, p. 10)

In the vast theoretical literature of critical pedagogy, issues of material, social, political, and cultural modes of production with such related topics as class, gender, race, and popular culture as critical social formations have been analysed during the past decades (Darder et al. 2003; McLaren and Kincheloe 2007; Macrine 2009). However, there have been only a few attempts so far to try to capture the effects of the rapidly growing field of digital production with its ever-evolving technologies, ideologies, and social codes – of course with some notable exceptions (see Giroux 2000a, 2004; Kellner 1995, 2004; Peters and Lankshear 1996; Lankshear and Knobel 2003).

In the debate, three general expectations about digital media as a 'teaching machine' can be discerned: threats (or even fears), promises, and possibilities. First, new information and communication technologies have been seen as threats from the point of view of their implicit technical rationality, 'technological determinism' and covert features of alienation. As Henry Giroux and Susan Searls Giroux (2004, p. 268) have put it, the central threat is not what new technologies enable, 'but that such technologies, when not shaped by ethical considerations, collective debate, and dialogical approaches, lose whatever potential they might have for linking education to critical thinking and learning to democratic social change'. In other words, 'the real issue is whether such technology in its various pedagogical uses ... is governed by a technocratic rationality that undermines human freedom and democratic values' (ibid.). These fears were explicated early on by the German philosopher Martin Heidegger in his critique of enframing and Herbert Marcuse in his critique of technocracy (see Thomson 2003). Heidegger thought that the ultimate danger of technology does not lie in its possible breakdowns (nuclear disaster, climate change, and so on) but rather in the fact that technology does not fail but works smoothly and faultlessly in its own hermetic realm, making us think of ourselves as resources (see, for example, Heidegger 1982). To use Heidegger's idea, one could say that the ultimate fear is that the 'teaching machines' enhanced with information technology will work seamlessly together with technological rationality so that all emancipatory potential is finally lost.

In the present, so-called frictionless capitalism, alienation has a new name, that of 'Capitalism with a Subversive Face'. In the modern industrial capitalism alienation was something which characterised the loss of workers' autonomy, Taylorised work and mass production for profit, among other things. At the same time there was a certain balance of horror, between a worker and a capitalist (armed struggle, revolts, trade unions, contracts, an eight hour work day were all weapons against capitalist exploitation). Nowadays alienation has become something more: in the name of profit, competition, globalisation – you name it – people need to sell not only their labour power but also their enthusiasm, creativity, and availability 24/7. In other words, they need to train their personalities in order to serve the needs of postmodern corporations which try to swallow the Wikiworld into their own logic. Exemplary here are hackers whose idiosyncratic habits of thought and lifestyles fit well with the needs of high-tech corporations. As Žižek points out:

> the tension is no longer between my innermost idiosyncratic creative impulses and the Institution that either doesn't appreciate them or wants to crush them in order to 'normalize' me: what the superego-injunction of

> the postmodern Corporation (like Microsoft) targets is precisely this core of my idiosyncratic creativity – I become useless for them the moment I start loosing this 'imp of perversity', the moment I lose my 'counter-cultural' subversive edge and start to behave like a 'normal' mature subject. There thus emerges a strange alliance between the rebellious subversive core of my personality and the external Corporation. (Žižek 2007b, p. 232)

But, from the point of view of alienation, the difference is quite hard to catch: both instances of alienation, those based on manual labour power with nuts and bolts, or those based on creative brain work with bits and screens, are still about reducing humanity and personality into a thing, making a person another cog in the capitalist machinery.

For his part Herbert Marcuse saw technocracy as a political state in which 'technical considerations of imperialistic efficiency and rationality supersede the traditional standards of profitability and general welfare' (Marcuse 1941 cited in Thomson 2003, p. 61; see also Kellner 1998b). But what distinguishes Marcuse's critique of technology from Heidegger's and also from most of his peers around the Frankfurt School, was his insistence that technology also holds a promise if its instrumentality can be thought of differently. The idea is to modify technology by the abolition of class society and the principle of reducing people to things or mere resources to be optimised with maximal efficiency. For it is 'not only an ontological question of what technology is making of us; that question needs to be posed, to be sure, but we must also ask the political question of what we can make of technology' (Feenberg 1998). This line of thought is to be found in most critical educators who, in Marcuse's footsteps, 'reject the hype and pretensions of techno-utopias and techno-fixes to the problems of education and society' (Kellner 2004, p. 13), and instead want to examine critically and reflect on the uses of information and communication technologies together with progressive and transformative pedagogical theories.

On the other hand, digital technologies and their evolving applications have been seen as containing the promises and potential of a new public sphere and 'hyperpedagogy' (Dwight and Garrison 2003) to be formed in cyberspace with diverse digital learning tools; for some this has promised a new, enhanced active citizenship. Referring to the 2,500-year-old Western teleological, dogmatic metaphysics with predetermined and rational educational ends, technological enthusiasts demand that digital learning tools 'should free students to create their own unique essences in the learning process rather than have their essences proscribed by a teleological value system of predetermined fixed ends' (ibid., p. 724). The latter promise has also been seen in the rejuvenation of a Habermasian ideal communication (see Habermas 1981) consisting of open and free rational discussions in various web fora.

Diverse spheres of digitally mediated communication – wikispheres, blogospheres, podspheres, and so on – have the potential to enlarge and enhance educational expertise into new areas of learning such as private enterprise, consulting and digitally conducted distance education by using new information and communication technologies. Critical theorists have for their part called for new emancipatory skills and literacies needed in comprehending various digital spaces and incorporating them in the settings of radical politico-social transformation and educational change. In terms of new possibilities, Kahn and Kellner (2006) have maintained that

> people should be helped to advance the multiple technoliteracies that will allow them to understand, critique, and transform the oppressive social and cultural conditions in which they live, as they become ecologically-informed, ethical, and transformative subjects as opposed to objects of technological domination and manipulation. This requires producing multiple oppositional literacies for critical thinking, reflection, and the capacity to engage in the creation of discourse, cultural artifacts, and political action amidst widespread technological revolution. Further, as active and engaged subjects arise through social interactions with others, a notion of convivial technologies must come to be a part of the kinds of technoliteracy that a radical reconstruction of education now seeks to cultivate.

Besides these questions of skills and literacy, only a few have dared to ask the substantial questions pertaining to the critical or even revolutionary potential of social media. In the following we want to probe this question by using the effects of Wikipedia and other wikis like it as examples. Wiki software seems to promise almost limitless global open collaboration in terms of content production, discussion and argumentation, and thus ideally exemplifies the Habermasian potential of digital technology. However, we need to look further into the depths of the nature of such technology in order to see how the much-hyped promise of wikis and other types of social media interacts with the real world's structural constraints and conflicts. In a nutshell, it is not the form but the content – what is said and why – that is crucial in evaluating digital media's effects, its promises and perils in terms of global justice. Consequently, the analysis of digital media in the context of communication and educational theory has to be intertwined with an analysis of critical political economy.

Wikipedia, the Free Encyclopedia

Wikipedia is a free encyclopedia in the sense of 'free speech': anyone is free to read, write, modify, redistribute Wikipedia articles (provided that the redistributed articles are given the same freedom). Started in 2001, the English language version of Wikipedia contains (September 2009) more than 3,000,000 articles and is constantly among the top ten of most visited web sites globally. The Wikipedia project is maintained by the non-profit Wikimedia Foundation that relies on donations for its finances. Wikipedia, together with its sister projects like Wikibooks, Wikimedia Commons and Wikiversity, is commonly cited as the most prominent example of the success of open collaboration. One of the key reasons for the success is the freedom of Wikipedia: the contents are licensed under the copyleft GFDL license which guarantees that contributions will always be available to everyone. Another is the radical openness of the editorial process, with the possibility to contribute anonymously, even though the process favours contributions from registered users so that vandalism can be prevented.
(http://www.wikipedia.org)

Although our book's topic is new digital literacies in the seemingly fancy world of new information and communications technologies, we have tried to keep the global increase of social, economic and educational inequalities firmly in mind. And as our frame of reference is the political economy of communication and media technologies and the critical sociology of education, we study these inequalities especially from the point of view of young people – those of us who inherit the world. Therefore we want to remind ourselves and our readers at the outset that even today there are over 100 million children who lack primary education: 55 per cent of them are girls. Wandering around – both literally and metaphorically – in the Mall of America, in one of the largest shopping paradises in the world, it can be hard to realise or remember that, according to UNESCO statistics, almost 800 million people aged 15 and over are still without basic literacy skills. Thus, the choice of writing about new information and communication technologies, whether in the traditional sense or in the sense of social media, already reveals a possible bias. Although we want to write critically and against the grain, the old saying 'the West and the rest' is highly illustrative, as we hope to show in what follows. And yet two more sobering facts: only one-sixth of the world's population uses the Internet on a regular basis. Where are these people? If you point to the affluent countries on the world map, you also point to the countries with the most Internet users. Basically, it is as simple as that.

Our Point of View: A Critical Paradigm of Education

Now that self-education and fraternal education are becoming more general, the teacher must, in the form he now normally assumes, become almost redundant. Friends anxious to learn, who want to acquire knowledge of something together, can find in our age of books a shorter and more natural way than 'school' and 'teacher' are.

(Nietzsche 1996, p. 353)

Friedrich Nietzsche wrote these words in the 1880s in his book for free spirits, *Human, All Too Human*. If Nietzsche's 'age of books' was replaced by 'age of lifelong learning', 'open learning', 'distance learning', 'co-operative learning', 'age of network learning' or 'new learning technologies', the above quotation would tell part of the story of contemporary educational thinking. Moreover, it summarises key ideas in the critical paradigm of education. A case in point is Ivan Illich and his ideas about deschooling society; they are a counterpoint to the present culture of learning and education as a commodity.

One basic belief in the critical paradigm of education is that learning and education are fundamentally social and political activities reaching across a spectrum from formal schooling to everyday life and ordinary activities. That is to say that learning is a centrally intersubjective human activity which belongs to and is part of our being in the world. Thus, there are at least three different views in the critical paradigm of education approaches which bear close resemblance to each other in their theoretical underpinnings.

The first one is developed by Bruner (1996). His seminal work in the area of cultural psychology is closely linked to Vygotsky's cultural historical theories of development. The second consists of those theories which emphasise that learning is a social phenomenon and plays a crucial role in different everyday- and work-related practices (Engeström and Middleton 1996). This includes the area of learning through apprenticeship (Lave and Wenger 1991; Kvale and Nielsen 1997). The third view can be called critical political economy of education, for researchers in this field are interested not merely in the sociality of learning as such, but also the ideological and political functions and consequences of learning and systemic education.

In this third view it is argued that social learning and education have to be understood as producing not only knowledge but also political subjects. Furthermore, as a form of cultural production, education and learning are 'implicated in the construction and organization of knowledge, desires, values, and social practices' (Giroux 1992, p. 3). In general, the critical studies in education approach tries to question and to redraw the old boundaries of educational research and practice. All these research orientations share the theoretical assumption that learning, like other human activities, always occurs in a certain place and time: in other words, learning is socially and politically situated, and its primary aim is to fight against oppressive social and political conditions, to further true democracy and to enhance cultural and political transformation (see McLaren and Jaramillo 2007; Giroux 2006). In addition, it is believed that learning, like other human activities, is historically and culturally bound.

Education in its diverse institutional forms has played a major role in creating the modern era. It is said that in the West, as well as in other post-industrial nations, we live in learning societies. Some theorists (Giroux 1995; Aittola et al. 1995) claim, however, that the modern legacy of schooling has begun to break down: the locus of significant learning experiences has shifted from school to peer-to-peer learning situations; from the formality of the classroom to the informality of diverse learning sites such as home, work, leisure-time and popular culture, and the Net. The proponents of this claim point out that because of current electronic information technologies, there is much more information available outside the classroom than inside.

These observations are, however, modern themselves and somewhat ahistorical. For if education and learning are viewed through a historical perspective, we see that it is neither informal learning nor learning outside the classroom but school-based learning that is a recent phenomenon (see Table 1.1). Historically, human beings have acquired most of their learning in their natural environments, that is, from learning to stay alive. In other words,

Table 1.1 History of Human Learning

Period	Premodern	Modern	Late Modern	Late Late-Modern
Form	Life itself	School	Life-long learning	Learning webs
Media	Tradition	Texts and informal learning	Networked examinations and life practices	Everyday life
Sphere	Local	National	National and global	Global and local
Function	Surviving	Knowing	Having	Being

people have learnt simply by living; life itself has been, and still is, the greatest educator (see also Antikainen et al. 1996). This applies equally to the Wikiworld with its abundance of information and communication.

Moreover, it is crucial to note the differences between the modern and the late modern eras of learning. Modernity was the time of school learning. The modern school was a bureaucratic organisation characterised by multiple standardised procedures (Kvale 1997). It was ruled by text-based learning and, especially, by formal and ritualised examination. It was the examination which, according to Foucault (1979, p. 192), was at the centre of procedures that constituted the individual, guaranteed the functions of distribution and classification, and, as a consequence, constant surveillance of pupils.

Largely, the school is the product of modern mass society, a response to the needs of industrialisation. Social and technological change have forced people as laborers to keep on learning – learning to have, know and think correctly – throughout their lives, to become lifelong learners who embrace the right attitudes for being modern and postmodern consumers. On the other hand, late modernity might mean different approaches to learning.

In late modernity, if seen as a time of collapsing moral and practical certainties (Bauman 1995), it could be assumed that learning will be defined through value rationality – in Weber's sense of the term – and characterised as a way of personal and social transformation more than through instrumental rationality and as a way to better competencies in the labour market. Similarly, as learning has shifted from the school to the various sites of networked everyday life, learning and pedagogy will be defined, using Giroux's (1994, p. x) words, as 'the creation of public sphere, one that brings people together in a variety of sites to talk, exchange information, listen, feel their desires, and expand their capacities for joy, love, solidarity, and struggle'. As we shall see, this is the picture Illich draws in his idea of convivial institutions.

In their current forms, it might be that schools no longer belong to the order of things in the late modern era, and are about to vanish from the map of human affairs, 'like a face drawn in sand at the edge of the sea', to paraphrase Foucault's (1994, p. 387) prediction about the future of human beings as an object of inquiry. This at least is Illich's standpoint in his *Deschooling Society* (1971). Before turning to some of Illich's central arguments important to our own thinking about the schooled society, and ways of deschooling it (through learning webs and a new notion of human being), we will describe some of the key points in his general educational thinking. First and foremost, Illich is a utopian thinker. Utopia, as u-topos, refers to a time or place which does not and never will exist. That is both the tragedy and hope of all utopias and utopian thinkers. Along with Paulo Freire, Illich was also one of the most radical political and social thinkers in the second half of the twentieth century. His aim was to analyse the institutional structures of industrialised society and to provide both rigorous criticism and a set of alternative concepts.

Illich's basic claim is that not only learning and education but also Western societies in general have become schooled. He describes this as the Western tendency to institutionalise the teaching of values. People have become dependent not only on school but also on other bureaucratic agencies of modern capitalistic societies: the consumer-family, the party, the army, the church, the media. According to him, all modern conveniences have hidden curricula designed to make people believe that they are essential services for people. Thus, he is a deconstructionist in the sense that he is ready to abolish schools as we know them and deschool a whole society. He is also a conservative in the sense that he does not believe in progress through schooling. Quite the contrary: in his view education leads 'to physical pollution, social polarization and psychological impotence'. His devaluing of modern institutions can be described as nomadic postmodernism, the basis for neo-Marxist criticism of Illich as a conservative.

According to Paula Allman (1988, pp. 90–1), Illich does not distinguish between the symptoms and the cause of the problem. That is, he wrongly locates the cause within schools and other institutions rather than within the socio-economic superstructure of capitalist societies. The neglect of material conditions and their ideological masking creates even more social divisions and inequalities. Furthermore, Illich's ideas about learning webs might work well in a socialistic order, but in market economies, says Allman, they are only piecemeal tactics which lead 'to securing further privilege for the dominant groups in these societies'. Illich himself wants to remind his critics about the fact that modern superstructures have effectively penetrated our lifeworlds and become major employers and benefactors of society. That is why Marxists fail to explain the triumph of the capitalist consumer society: the worker has profited from it and 'has a great deal more to lose than his chains' (Fromm 1970, p. 30). This, and the fact that schools are a form of industry, is often overlooked by neo-Marxists who argue that the process of deschooling must be postponed until other disorders are corrected. However, Illich (1996) has said that he has been misunderstood. Rather than deschooling society, he wanted to use the term 'disestablishment of schools' and reminds us to be alert when learning needs and demands are mentioned in the media.

Illich's approach resembles that of Nietzsche (1996) who, in *Human, All Too Human*, says that by means of school, rulers win the gifted poor over to their side. Teachers, above all, become members of the rulers' intellectual court by their unconscious striving for higher culture. Modern critics, because of their faith in progress through the sciences and emancipation of humans, do not share Illich's notion of late modernism aiming at abolishing all institutions, whether economical, administrative, ideological or political. In this sense Illich's criticism applies both to capitalism and socialism. The natural framework for Illich's approach, then, is the well-known social theoretical opposition between the system and the lifeworld, elaborated by Habermas (1989) in his theory of communicative action. Roughly speaking, Habermas's central argument is that the economic and administrative systems of modern societies are the primary conditions of colonisation of the lifeworld, which, in turn, is the source of social integration, symbolic reproduction and socialisation.

Surprisingly or not, Illich is a learning optimist, for he separates learning from teaching and schooling, from grade advancement and good behaviour, and from obedience and education. Thus, Illich's views do not reduce to any simple definition, they do not fit into any narrow ideological frame: they escape all trivialised readings through ready-made lenses. Illich maintains that learning belongs to a particular person and to that person only; it is one's right and one's duty. Thus, this position makes him, along with his learning theory, a proponent of an individualistic philosophy of education. His individualism is, however, socially conscious, for, as his theory of learning can be interpreted, individual actions form the basis for the emancipation of human beings; a genuine change is always based on one particular being's actions. In his individualism, Illich is also a Nietzschean free spirit. He says that school makes human beings abdicate the responsibility for their own learning and growth, and, in addition, makes many commit a kind of spiritual suicide. What, then, would better define his attitude towards the task of learning and self-transformation than Nietzsche's (1996, p. 379) aphorism 282: 'The teacher a necessary evil. – As few people as possible between the productive spirit and the spirits who hunger and receive!' Illich's utopia is turning out to be more of a topical scenario for our so-called information age than anyone imagined. Illich's learning web metaphor is in itself interesting. It represents nicely the current trend that it is as if all the best minds in education are found in the virtual world of the World Wide Web.

The point of departure in Illich's thinking is the idea of unlimited access to learning. In his words, '[T]he most radical alternative to school would be a network or service which gave each man [and woman, our addition] the same opportunity to share his [and her, our addition] current concern with others motivated by the same concern' (Illich 1971, p. 19). This requires 'the return of initiative and accountability for learning to the learner or his most immediate tutor' (ibid., p. 16). Illich thus wants to correct the common mistake that learning is the exclusive result of teaching, rather than that most learning occurs outside schools:

> Everyone learns how to live outside school. We learn to speak, to think, to love, to feel, to play, to curse, to politic, and to work without interference

from a teacher. Even children who are under a teacher's care day and night are no exceptions to the rule. Orphans, idiots, and schoolteachers' sons learn most of what they learn outside the 'educational' process planned for them. (ibid., pp. 28–9)

Nowadays, this is a commonplace for many educators. Studies in educational anthropology have shown that even in educational settings, in schools, there are 'extracurricular', non-academic and informal activities going on all the time: different clubs, events, meetings, projects, sports events, informal relationships, dating and romance (see Peshkin 1994). In his phenomenology of schools, Illich identifies several underlying assumptions, or hidden curricula of schooling that constrain unlimited access to learning. From a global viewpoint Illich sees that most parents cannot afford to provide a childhood for their offspring. Furthermore, those who can, feel that it is a burden, not a blessing. Illich sees childhood, as Westerners know it, as a construction of the nineteenth-century bourgeoisie. Furthermore, a teacher–pupil relationship is based on the belief that culture must be transmitted from the older generation to the younger: schools do not fulfil this task because 'pupils have never credited teachers for most of their learning' (Illich 1971, p. 29).

In addition, full-time attendance at school 'tends to make a total claim on the time and energies of its participants' (ibid., p. 30). This makes teachers into custodians, moralist-preachers, and therapists. Illich argues that teachers' powers mentioned above, along with attendance rules, create an enclave which is more primitive, magical and total than the everyday world of Western culture. In this magic zone, distinctions between morality, legality and personal worth collapse into one and every student's mistake is seen as a multiple offence.

Illich also analyses the broader hidden curriculum of schooling. This analysis reveals that schooling serves as a rite of initiation into a growth-oriented consumer society creating 'the myths of schooling'. The myth of unending consumption is strengthened by the idea that teaching produces learning (compared to the idea of learning by doing or participating in a meaningful setting).

Learning is understood as a product that has the same structure as other merchandise. Schools are learning factories which produce demand for school learning. The myth of measurement of values says that everything can be measured, from personal growth, happiness and intelligence to the development of nations and progress toward peace. Furthermore, education and learning are defined as consumer goods, as merchandise that is sold and bought on the school market. Consumer parents, who can afford it, make education investments and read college ratings in order to measure the exchange value of their money. Schooling at all levels is big business.

The myth of self-perpetuating progress emphasises that the number of persons effectively treated by a teacher measures the success of schooling. We have pupil-hours, study points and credits, and other statistics, which allow competition and comparison between pupils, schools, areas, and nations. This is the mythical ideal of today's political rhetoric of education. In the present situation, schooling is like an obligatory lottery machine. Children are allowed to play, but the game is not fair. Those who 'choose' the right parents as well as the right race, culture and nation, that is, the family with social, educational and economic wealth and capital, are more advantaged than others, and collect the prizes in the fields of constant educational competition.

Schooling is not only the new world religion, with its attendant curses and blessings, but also one of the fastest-growing markets in the world. Thus, schooling is a form of alienation, for it creates an illusion that students are the creators of their own wisdom, although they are only objects of the knowledge industry, in which knowledge 'is conceived as a commodity put on the market in school' (Illich 1971, p. 47). According to Illich, the school is the main evil, the manipulative institution which shapes people's vision of reality. The school 'enslaves more profoundly and more systematically'; it 'touches us so intimately that none of us can expect to be liberated from it by something else' (ibid.). There are, however, other instances with the same functions and their own hidden curricula: family life, military service, health care and media. Hence, Illich splits institutions into manipulative and 'convivial', and offers a classification of different institutions depending on their totality or openness.

On the manipulative side are institutions like law enforcement, the army, prisons, mental hospitals, nursing homes and orphanages. Membership in these socially or psychologically addictive institutions is achieved coercively, 'by forced commitment or selective service' (ibid., p. 54). Convivial or spontaneous institutions, on the other hand, are like telephone links, subway lines, mail routes, public markets and free exchange of ideas. This type of institution is like a network which facilitates communication and co-operation among free agents. Illich sketches a picture of the public place where learning and other kinds of activities would flourish – naturally without charge:

> There could be tool shops, libraries, laboratories, and gaming rooms. Photo labs and offset presses would allow neighborhood newspapers to flourish. Some storefront learning centers could contain viewing booths for closed-circuit television, others could feature office equipment for use and for repair. The jukebox or the record player would be commonplace, with some specializing in classical music, others in international folk tunes, others in jazz. Film clubs would compete with each other and with commercial television. Museum outlets could be networks for circulating exhibits of works of art, both old and new, originals and reproductions, perhaps administered by the various metropolitan museums. (ibid., p. 84)

As the above quote clearly shows, Illich's thinking is holistic or multidisciplinary in nature. He is not only suggesting an educational reform with the idea of convivial institution but, at the same time, working in the fields of urban planning, architecture and social policy. Modern schooling reflects the consumer society as both cause and consequence. It makes learning and education into commodities that can be marketed, sold, bought, consumed, wasted and recycled; teaching becomes a relation between a supplier and a consumer even though in a quite paradoxical way: 'it guaranteed the movement of knowledge from the teacher to the pupil, but it extracted from the pupil a knowledge destined and reserved for the teacher' (Foucault 1979, p. 187). All this is made to happen in various kinds of learning institutions. Nor is the ideology of schooling restricted to childhood. As Illich points out, it applies equally to adulthood in the form of lifelong learning. Illich (1971, p. 69), obviously, believes neither in the ideas of lifelong learning nor open learning environments:

> Now the teacher-therapists go on to propose life-long educational treatment as the next step. The style of this treatment is under discussion: Should it take the form of continued adult classroom attendance? Electronic ecstasy? Or periodic sensitivity sessions? All educators are ready to conspire to push out the walls of the classroom, with the goal of transforming the entire culture into a school.

The spontaneous use of institutions opens up the possibility of different learning webs, including Illich's core idea of unlimited access to learning. There are three preconditions for the creation of a deschooled society in Illich's utopia: changes in the arrangements of learning, new aims for the educational system and changes in teachers' roles. Thus, the arrangements of learning, which could give each human being the same opportunity to share their current concerns with others similarly concerned, are (Illich 1971, p. 103):

1. Reference services to educational objects as a system 'to liberate access to things by abolishing the control which persons and institutions now exercise over their educational values'.
2. Skill exchanges as an adjustment 'to liberate the sharing of skills by guaranteeing freedom to teach or exercise them on request'.
3. Peer matching as a communication network which liberates 'the critical and creative resources of people by returning to individual persons the ability to call and hold meetings'.
4. Reference services to educators-at-large as a directory 'to liberate the individual from the obligation to shape his [or her] expectations to the services offered by any established profession by providing him [or her] with the opportunity to draw on the experience of his [or her] peers and to entrust himself [or herself] to the teacher, guide, adviser, or healer of his [or her] choice'.

A good educational arrangement as a convivial system would, then, provide everyone who wants to learn at any time in their life with access to available resources; it would empower people to share their knowledge; and it would give an opportunity to people to present an issue to the public whenever it is necessary. To accomplish the task of deschooling society certain types of teachers are also needed. The first type is composed of network administrators, who would build and operate diverse learning networks. The second consists of pedagogues, who would facilitate learning and help people to find their own paths in the networks. The third is composed of educational leaders, *primus inter pares*, whose task would be to create dialogical educational relationships. This latter kind of educational relationship is, according to Aristotle in his *Nicomachean Ethics*, like a moral type of friendship: 'it makes a gift, or does whatever it does, as to a friend'. Thomas Aquinas characterises this relationship as an act of love and mercy. Illich says that it is always a mutual luxury, a form of leisure for the teacher and for the pupil.

In addition to the changes in the arrangements of learning, the aims of the educational system and the teachers' role, new attitudes and, what is of importance, a new conception of human being is also needed. Illich suggests that the above-mentioned learning webs should lean not on technology but on co-operation, caring, and sharing of knowledge and skills between people. Furthermore, Illich claims that changes in the role and use of institutions are not possible without a dramatic change in current worldviews, conceptions of human being and the functions of human beings in the world. Currently we are living in a technological utopia in which it is believed that all the problems created in modernity, social as well as political and educational, are susceptible to a technical solution and qualitative improvements are possible through technological development. This is the dogma of institutionalising values. According to Illich, we have to move to another utopia, which Erich Fromm (1971) calls humanistic radicalism. Fromm's words are worth quoting at length:

Humanistic radicalism is radical questioning guided by insight into the dynamics of man's nature; and by concern for man's growth and full unfolding. ... All this means that humanist radicalism questions every idea and every institution from the standpoint of whether it helps or hinders man's capacity for greater aliveness and joy. This is not the place to give lengthy examples for the kind of common-sensical premises that are questioned by humanist radicalism. ... I want to mention only a few like the modern concept of 'progress,' which means the principle of ever-increasing production, consumption, timesaving, maximal efficiency and profit, and calculability of economic activities without regard to their effect on the quality of living and the unfolding of man; or the dogma that increasing consumption makes man happy, that the management of large-scale enterprises must necessarily be bureaucratic and alienated; that the aim of life is having (and using), not being; that reason resides in the intellect and is split from the affective life; that the newer is always better than the older; that radicalism is the negation of tradition; that the opposite of 'law and order' is lack of structure. In short, that the ideas and categories that have arisen during the development of modern science and industrialism are superior to those of all former cultures and indispensable for the progress of the human race.

Illich's new conception of human beings can be translated into a less metaphysical language of learning. In Table 1.2, two conceptions of learning are opposed. The table also shows some of the thinkers who have elaborated these conceptions. Illich's conception is in the right-hand column, with other critical humanists.

Here we further explicate Erich Fromm's (1996, p. 16) distinction, in which he separates two concepts, those of having and being, which refer to two fundamental but distinct modes of experience and learning. Learning as having, on the one hand, reflects the archaic idea of incorporating a thing in order to possess it. Fromm says that the attitude inherent in consumerism – and, we might add, schooling and the Net as commodity and the marketplace in the spirit of Illich – is that of incorporating, 'of swallowing the whole world' (ibid., p. 27). On the other hand, learning as being refers to internally motivated learning, learning without any other purpose than ethically meaningful self-trans-formation, and learning as an end in itself.

It seems as if Illich's utopia drew society as an island of free spirits sharing opinions and ideas in an Eden-like purity, without social powers, social divisions or other modern pollutants. This is, of course, a caricature of Illich's utopian or nomadic postmodernism.

Table 1.2 Two Conceptions of Learning

Learning as ...	
Consumer good	An end in itself (Kant)
Having	Being (Fromm), sharing and caring
Political bargaining and rhetoric	Self-transformation (Foucault)
Manifestation of instrumental rationality	An act of love and mercy (both eros and agape) (Thomas Aquinas)
Domination	The practice of freedom (Freire)
Surveillance and social status quo	Social criticism (Apple)
Engineering and economic utility	Askesis, experiment, pleasure (hooks)
And taking place in ...	
Manipulative institutions	'Convivial' institutions (Illich)

Zygmunt Bauman (1995) claims that, unlike in modernity, in late modernity people are left alone with their moral dilemmas. Modernity was the era of philosophers as moral legislators, preachers as ethical experts and teachers as therapists, whereas late modernity demands that people take care of their own moral decisions, ethical dilemmas and educational tasks. In postmodernity, there is no longer a solid foundation of morality in the form of institutions, grand narrative or ideas. In Bauman's (ibid., 43) words, 'it is possible now, nay inevitable, to face the moral issues point-blank, in all their truth, as they emerge from the life experience of men and women, and as they confront moral selves in all their irreparable and irredeemable ambivalence'.

In our interpretation this is the intellectual landscape in which a thinker like Illich can be understood. There are, however, a number of problems in Illich's thinking. In the same way as other utopias, Illich's individualism and radical humanism are based on a too-positive image of human beings. They forget that people are capable of evil (as Goethe says: 'that there is no crime of which one cannot imagine oneself to be the author') and inclined to laziness. Along with other utopians, Illich is a true believer in fair play; he believes in a just society (in the manner of John Rawls (1971)). He does not want to take into account the evident fact that all social institutions, no matter how sophisticated in design, contain freeloaders such as learning consultants, therapists of different kinds and degree hunters unconcerned about actual learning. Furthermore, his model assumes that everybody wins and nobody loses, a practical impossibility in human affairs.

Although Illich does speak about social institutions and their powers over individual learners, he, like other utopians, does not analyse the concept of power in depth. He believes that people are inherently good, that learning webs are democratic in themselves, and that people in them work on an equal basis. Like all good utopians, he also believes that people are ready for the proposed changes, that they are willing to adjust their attitudes and behaviour. Moreover, he assumes that they will act like autonomous learners and use their reason with courage, as Kant demanded.

Illich would not be a utopian thinker unless he took his ideas to extremes. He seems to think that schooled society, devoted to 'the god of Consumership' (Postman 1996, p. 33), is fanatic and hegemonic; it offers no alternatives to its grand narrative of competition through schooling. Keeping these reservations in mind when reading Illich, it is still possible, we believe, to face the moral issue of education, schooling and learning straight on, in all its truth as it emerges from the life experience of men and women, teachers and administrators, children and politicians.

Thus, a close reading of Illich's prophetic and utopian book also poses nowadays rarely mentioned questions: How to be an autonomous learner when autonomy revolves around the educational techniques of power? How to break free from the oppression of the system when there is no oppression anymore, only free enterprise and happy learning? In the spirit of critical education, Illich invites us to ask: What are schools for? What is the reason for schooling? Is there any reason? What are the forms of counternarrative in a world of perpetual freedom of educational choices? With these questions in mind, it is possible to develop a new sensitivity for seeing the commonplaces of education as something strange and odd, and to develop a sharpened sense of educational reality.

2
DIGITAL LITERACY AND POLITICAL ECONOMY

At a certain stage of their development, the material productive forces of society come in conflict with the existing relations of production, or – what is but a legal expression for the same thing – with the property relations within which they have been at work hitherto. From forms of development of the productive forces these relations turn into their fetters. Then begins an epoch of social revolution. With the change of the economic foundation the entire immense superstructure is more or less rapidly transformed. In considering such transformations a distinction should always be made between the material transformation of the economic conditions of production, which can be determined with the precision of natural science, and the legal, political, religious, aesthetic or philosophic – in short, ideological forms in which men become conscious of this conflict and fight it out. Just as our opinion of an individual is not based on what he thinks of himself, so can we not judge of such a period of transformation by its own consciousness; on the contrary, this consciousness must be explained rather from the contradictions of material life, from the existing conflict between the social productive forces and the relations of production. No social order ever perishes before all the productive forces for which there is room in it have developed; and new, higher relations of production never appear before the material conditions of their existence have matured in the womb of the old society itself. Therefore mankind always sets itself only such tasks as it can solve; since, looking at the matter more closely, it will always be found that the task itself arises only when the material conditions of its solution already exist or are at least in the process of formation.

(Marx 1859)

An image may be '1. An optical representation of a real object, or 2. A mental picture of something not real or not present' (http://en.wiktionary.org/wiki/image): the image of the information society is like the *persona* of a human being which presents itself in full view only to hide something else. Nevertheless, does an image reveal the truth insofar as it has its causal history and its consequences? What if the questioning, the *polemos*, of the information society – like any other society – has to be done precisely on the level of its image, its influence, mobility and speed? What if the image of the information society as a 'logic of networks', 'informationalism' and 'risk society' is true, corresponding to the reality of wealthy First World countries like Finland, a country with one of the highest rates of suicide in the world? The image responds with a wry smile, and tells us that we should not be so dense: Truth is relative, the truth for or by someone. For whom is the contemporary society an information society or a network society? What is its price to humanity?

If we ask who we are and what characterises the times in which we are living, one of the prominent answers is the notion of risk society. We live in a time when modern societies have progressed to a stage where, as Beck (1995, p. 16) points out, the social, political, economic and personal risks are beyond the control of traditional institutions. At first, risks are created without paying much attention, then they rise to the focus of political discussion, shadowing other conflicts and clashes. With the inevitability of contemporary economy-driven development, the risk society is not an option to be chosen, but an inevitable consequence of modernisation (ibid., p. 17.) The same goes for the logic of networks and 'informationalism that is replacing industrialism as the hegemonic form' (Castells 2000, p. 139); you have to participate in the networks or face extinction. The frontline of information society is not between workers and capitalists but between a netocratic elite and the mass of passive consumers, 'the consumtariat' (Žižek 2004a, p. 192).

The fundamental difference between the netocracy and consumers is 'that the former controls its own production of desire, whereas the latter obeys the orders of the former. Hence there is vital symbolic value for netocracy in continually signifying in one's choice of lifestyle that one is independent of consumptive production of manipulated desire, and thereby indicating one's social distance from the vulgar masses' (Bard and Söderqvist 2002, p. 141).

Netocrats travel to places without a tourist industry, listen to music that is not available from any record company, get their entertainment from subscription channels or websites that neither carry adverts nor advertise their own existence, and consumer goods and services that are never mentioned in the media and which are therefore unknown to the masses. This lifestyle can never be fixed: it will always be in a process of constant change. When the netocrats tire of one desire and the experience has lost its value, they can always throw it to the masses – recreating it for the consumtariat with the help of adverts – and this also has its economic advantages. But whatever is reserved for the time being for the netocracy will always be unknown, incomprehensible and out of reach for the consumtariat. (ibid.)

Furthermore, it is maintained that to recognise and to understand this and other dialectics of the present era is to be 'reflexively modern'. If the reflexivity of modernisation is seen as a normative or pedagogical – that is, political – concept, we enter the field of politics of recognition: who recognises what and why? We are inclined to think that at this state of modernity reflexivity is flawed by any measure of social equality and global justice. In its current forms reflexivity produces mere social frigidity and competition between the people of the West. The risk society is a risk first and foremost because common sense, political decision-making and philosophical reflection have not kept up with the ecological, sociological and ideological changes – not to mention new ethical demands in terms of equality and caretaking. Corporative and militarist globalisation has totally evaded these issues in its empty discourses of open markets and free competition. If these socio-political sea changes are mentioned, they are used to justify the inevitability of the US and World Trade Organisation (WTO)-controlled direction of the global order. But does the notion of risk society make it possible to change current socio-political structures? How does it measure up to the actual (absolute, substantial, real, material) events and forms of alterity that emerge outside the Western sphere, or to the real anomalies of the West itself (including structural violence, drugs, medicalisation, depression, exhaustion …)?

What reflexive modernity can embrace is the steady individualisation and atomisation of the human being; we are doomed to become individuals forced to 'design and re-design' (Beck 1995, p. 27) our own autobiographies, especially with regard to work, where the world is divided into winners and losers (Castells 2000, p. 147). This individual is no longer the autonomous subject of enlightenment, but rather a heteronomous postmodern chameleon and nomad, rearranging him- or herself and his or her identity according to the situation, always slipping from the pincers of totalising systems. Economic production, the individual as a subject and politics are all *ad hoc* projects, as explained by Gilles Deleuze; reality itself is continual becoming, and humans the machinistic realisation nodes of non-subjective affects, drives and desires. Reality contains a virtual aspect that connects seemingly solid everyday objects to a necessary but invisible web of connections, influxions and investments (Deleuze and Guattari 1993, 1987).

Staging the Information Society

In order to overcome these anomalies, reflexive modernity invents the idea of 'reinventing the political'. This is the call to which the idea of digital social media responds with a promise to reorganise the political and breathe new life into democracy. Information technology contains a huge promise: 'Technology will make it increasingly difficult for the state to control the information its people receive. ... The Goliath of totalitarianism will be brought down by the David of the microchip', as Ronald Reagan observed in 1989 (quoted in Kalathil and Boas 2003), long before Al Gore allegedly invented the Internet. The crucial thing is not the availability of information but the relationship between information as reality and ourselves:

> As game programmers instead of game players, the creators of testimony rather than the believers in testament, we begin to become aware of just how much of our reality is open source and up for discussion. So much of what seemed like impenetrable hardware is actually software and ripe for reprogramming. The stories we use to understand the world seem less like explanations and more like collaborations. (Rushkoff 2003, p. 37)

The 'interactive renaissance' predicted by Rushkoff (ibid.3, p. 39) promises the return of the political:

> Interactivity, both as an allegory for a healthier relationship to cultural programming, and as an actual implementation of a widely accessible authoring technology, reduces our dependence on fixed narratives while giving us the tools and courage to develop narratives together. ... We have witnessed together the wizard behind the curtain. We can all see, for this moment anyway, how so very much of what we have perceived of as reality is, in fact, merely social construction. More importantly, we have gained the ability to enact such wizardry ourselves.

The promise of social media is that technological innovation is giving voice to a plurality that was previously choked by the bottlenecks of 'broadcasting'. In harmony with the logic of networks, the ailment and the cure stem from the same root: the centralised subject of totalitarianism and authoritarianism is replaced by a multitude of voices generated by the immateriality of work in the information society. As Hardt and Negri (2000) point out, immaterial production makes ownership superfluous and gives the workers the possibility of mastering their own social order. A dream is born; the dream of cybercommunism, where the networked subjects interact in producing intangible bits in a cornucopian community unlimited by the scarce resources of a material world (see also Merten 2000).

This dream is preceded by the idea of a frictionless capitalism. Corporations outsource risks, both economical and ecological, to consumers who also work as co-designers of the new products. In addition this means individualisation of corporate risks, a phenomenon sociologist Richard Sennett (2003) has labelled as the 'cd-rom economy'. In the centre there is a laser which reads the most essential information needed to run economic operations properly. In the present 'lean' organisations these lasers consist of a group of executives and operative leaders who rule, make decisions, set tasks and assess the results.

Reinventing the political gives two new directions for 'creative and autonomous' action. First, it means the overcoming of the old left–right classification, and, second, the birth of the politics of the everyday or biopolitics. While class-consciousness as an empirical experience has, indeed, faded in many First World countries, class structures have not gone away. Politics is no longer an attempt to make decisions according to an analysis of these positions (left versus right, working class versus capitalists) but rather applies to a world categorised beyond the old distinctions. The basic questions are: How do you deal with uncertainty, foreigners, living together (Beck 1995, p. 65)? These questions are faced in the choppy waters of everyday life, far beyond the familiar shores of political parties. Immense possibilities for economic and political action (double-dealing, freeloading, being an entrepreneur) and unsatisfied needs (New Age, spiritualism, porn, reality-reality) are created alongside longing for a new clarity and hardness (extreme sports, self-mutilation, anorexia, obsession with health and food, religious and atheist fundamentalism). Reflexive modernity does not imply the fulfilment of the broken tradition of enlightenment, a renaissance of the people and its freedoms, but rather a renaissance of a staging of the people and the staging of a renaissance of the people (ibid., p. 66).

'Information society' is properly understood as the name for this charade, the reality TV or, better yet, reality YouTube of everyday life, where we try to act as if we were not acting. Reality TV is at its best when it stages a real competition or takes home the advertising money while someone presents the unorthodox choices they made in their everyday life. For instance, they might have chosen not to wear underwear ever again or to find a suitable sexual partner for their parents. Being extravagant and being a freak is tolerated as long as it does not disturb the peace of the consumtariat; what if somebody decided to be a Nazi or a racist? As Žižek (2002a, p. 542) asks, 'Can one imagine a better summary of what the freedom of choice effectively amounts to in our liberal societies?'

Demos and Actuality

The theory of reflexive modernity does recognise some of the problems of postmodernity and the need for new conceptual and pragmatic models, but the tools it offers (the politics of the everyday, creativity, new solutions to new problems, new single-issue movements) are not sufficient to shake the structures of economic production or social life. The liberal system is by definition ecumenical, listening to every group (from feminists to fair trade activists) equally and patiently, as long as these groups do not threaten democracy itself. All critique is allowed, even welcomed, as long as the plethora of critiques is under the umbrella of 'critique of globalisation' and without any meaningful unity. We have created a politics without the political, where all you can do is either stay in (to form alliances and try to be close to the core of decision-making) or form yet another social movement and join the queue.

What both of these possibilities neglect is the level of 'concrete universality' where a single-issue movement no longer stands only for itself but for the whole, the society as a totality:

> the members of the *demos* (those with no firmly determined place in the hierarchical social edifice) presented themselves as the representatives, the stand-ins, for the whole of society, for the true universality ('we – the "nothing," not counted in the order – are the people, we are all, against others who stand only for their particular privileged interest'). Political conflict proper thus involves the tension between the structured social body, where each part has its place, and the part of no-part, which unsettles this order on account of the empty principle of universality, of the principled equality of all men qua speaking beings, what Étienne Balibar calls *égaliberté*. Politics proper thus always involves a kind of short circuit between the universal and the particular; it involves the paradox of a singular that appears as a stand-in for the universal, destabilizing the 'natural' functional order of relation in the social body. The *singulier universal* is a group that, although without any fixed place in the social edifice (or, at best, occupying a subordinated place), not only demands to be heard on equal footing with the ruling oligarchy or aristocracy (that power) but, even more, presents itself as the immediate embodiment of society as such, in its universality, against the particular power interests of aristocracy or oligarchy. (Žižek 1998, pp. 988–9)

If the multitude of movements acts as a critique of power and as 'resistance', what happens when power is no longer criticised or resisted, but taken and used? As Žižek (2004a, p. 199) writes, the Zapatista leader 'Subcomandante Marcos' – also known as Rafael Guillén – who speaks for various critics of globalisation, is an important icon of resistance. But what happens when this masked man who speaks for the oppressed and knows the feelings of his people turns into a powerful president? *Vestibulia terrent*. The politics of multiple voices is faced with a dilemma: *ad hoc diversity* is by definition resistance, while the wielding of power necessarily turns into a totalitarianism that is forced to swallow the bitter pill offered by the World Bank, the International Monetary Fund (IMF) and the WTO.

Does the dilemma of reflexive modernity also characterise the concept of information society? Does the notion also cover up its material roots? Does the information society contain a notion of freedom that is purely formal? In other words, does the information society exist in a vacuum created by ideological-economical necessities? Do we not need an information society of actual freedom, where the structure of the ideological setting, its material conditions and the nature of the subject can all be changed? Žižek (2002a, p. 544) defines formal freedom 'as freedom of choice within the coordinates of the existing power relations, while actual freedom designates the site of an intervention that undermines', contradicts and problematises these very co-ordinates. Thus an act of actual freedom breaks the seduction of symbolic order (Žižek 2001, p. 121). The idea of actual freedom demonstrates how what we used to call the information society (like any other form of society, a symbolic order) is lived and reproduced as if it were real, or at least in the process of becoming real. In this precise sense actual freedom refers to the social existence in which the expression 'as if' always already defines that which is only just becoming. Actual freedom thus draws a revolutionary line in which the future is at hand and 'we already are free while fighting for freedom, we already are happy while fighting for happiness, no matter how difficult the circumstances' (Žižek 2002a, p. 559).

Freedom is based on a misunderstanding: The king is still alive, but we act as if he was dead.

Political Economy and Digital Media

In studying actual freedom in more detail, we need the concepts of political economy, for the analysis has to be based on the properties of digital media and the collective uses that give them their distinctive character. An account of digital literacy guided by an understanding of digital technology will, in turn, direct attention to the overall features of the development of information societies. Insights into what we want to call strong digital literacy should imply a vision of what a desirable information society is all about. The *differentia specifica* of digital media – interactivity, multimodality and non-linearity, possibilities for recombination and perfect copying – are not neutral toward established forms of society. To take one example only, the convergence of media technologies made possible by digitalisation is rapidly changing the entire landscape of forms, use and ownership of the media. And when it comes to the concept of digital literacy there is a hegemonic struggle going on regarding its uses and definition. As Lankshear and Knobel (2005) characterise the two aspects of the current debate:

> First, currently prevailing views of digital literacy share in common the ideas that there is a 'thing' we can call digital literacy; 'it' is singular; its essence can be rendered as a standardised measurable competency – or unified set of more specific competencies and skills; and it comprises a 'truthcentric' ideal of information proficiency. Second, in the established world of conventional print-based literacy various agents and organisations take it upon themselves to define what literacy is, to teach it, measure it, assess it, and remediate it – in a word, to universalise and standardize it. Similarly, we find government bodies as well as non-governmental organisations like the Global Digital Literacy Council, the Educational Testing Service (ETS, USA), the International Society for Technology in Education (ISTE), and the OECD's [Organisation for Economic Co-operation and Development's]

Program for International Student Assessment (PISA) currently taking it upon themselves to do exactly the same in the area of digital literacy.

From the critical point of view, one can argue that digital literacy has been rapidly colonised by various international bodies as well as supranational and intergovernmental unions who use it as their tool to govern, or who, in Foucaultian vocabulary, practise 'governmentality'. The battle over definitions is one thing; another is an unprecedented concentration of media ownership as the key consequence of the digital revolution. In terms of political economy, 'the complex structure of power between states, capitalist markets and social groups has shifted to a great extent towards the interests of powerful private capitalist actors and institutions in what is often described as global civil society' (Wilkin 2002, p. 18). Thus, one obvious answer to the question of why a political economy perspective is needed when analysing digital literacy is that 'we are living at a particular historical juncture of unregulated capitalism with an overwhelming income reconcentration at the top' (McLaren 2000, p. 98), and as a consequence, power has shifted out of the public realm and into the realm of private corporations.

Simultaneously, the digital media have been celebrated as a tool that inevitably leads not only toward democratisation and the emergence of different kinds of grassroots civil society activities but also economic gains for all, at least in the new folklore of the global elite. As Zygmunt Bauman puts it, we ordinary people are made to believe by the fortunate, 'enlightened class' that

opening up and dynamiting all state-maintained dams will make the world a free place for everybody. According to such folkloristic beliefs, freedom (of trade and capital mobility, first and foremost) is the hothouse in which wealth would grow faster than ever before; and once the wealth is multiplied, there will be more of it for everybody. The poor of the world – whether old or new, hereditary or computer-made – would hardly recognize their plight in this folkloristic fiction. The media are the message, and the media through which establishment of the world-wide market is being perpetrated do not facilitate, but, on the contrary, preclude the promised 'trickle-down' effect. New fortunes are born, sprout and flourish in the virtual reality, tightly isolated from the old-fashioned rough-and-ready realities of the poor. The creation of wealth is on the way to finally emancipating itself from its perennial – constraining and vexing – connections with making things, processing materials, creating jobs and managing people. The old rich needed the poor to make and keep them rich. That dependency at all times mitigated the conflict of interest and prompted some effort, however tenuous, to care. The new rich do not need the poor any more. At long last the bliss of ultimate freedom is nigh. (Bauman 1998, pp. 71–2)

Digital literacy promises a leap to authorship, the transformation of 'receivers' into active creators, collaborators or authors of new media content. However, this promise is counteracted by contemporary large scale economic trends 'in which the market becomes the master template for all human affairs, ... a dystopian vision designed to affect almost every dimension of everyday life, including large cutbacks in social programs, freeing market forces from government regulations, and the ongoing privatization of government services, public goods, and non-commodified spheres' (Giroux 2003a, p. 468). As a result, information societies face an internal tension between the technology- and profit-driven information society agenda promoted by the international mega-companies and the richly varied agendas of the civil society representatives, including the hackers and hactivists who still today initiate groundbreaking technological developments. This internal tension is well portrayed in the declaration titled 'Shaping Information Societies for Human Needs' that was issued by the civil societies to the UN World Summit on the Information Society in Geneva 2003:

We are conscious that information, knowledge and the means of communication are available on a magnitude that humankind has never dreamt of in the past; but we are also aware that exclusion from access to the means of communication, from information and from the skills that are needed to participate in the public sphere, is still a major constraint, especially in developing countries. At the same time information and knowledge are increasingly being transformed into private resources which can be controlled, sold and bought, as if they were simple commodities and not the founding elements of social organization and development. Thus, as one of the main challenges of information and communication societies, we recognise the urgency of seeking solutions to these contradictions.

The notion of digital literacy is at the very heart of this tension. From the political economy perspective it is not enough to analyse and define (digital) literacy as a mere technique or a simple question of basic literacy taught in schools. As Lankshear and Knobel (2003, p. 5) point out in a Freirean tone, literacy is a form of political action and political acting in the world. In this sense to be (digitally) literate is 'to read the word and the world', that is, to analyse and understand the results and consequences of one's actions better than before in their socio-political context. And based on the new understanding of the world, to criticise and to change the world for the better.

Furthermore, as a politico-structural concept defining the character of the information societies to come, digital literacy contains the issues of authorship and ownership of information and thus invites a perspective of political economy (for a definition of the political economy of communication, see McChesney 1998; Wilkin 2002). The political economy of communication and digitalisation often refers to the issues of ownership and control of the means of communication, that is, to the issue of media concentration, and its effects on the structures of power that exist between states, capitalist markets, and various social groups seen in terms of class, gender, ethnicity, race and nation (Wilkin 2002, p. 20). The crucial point from a political economy perspective is that media concentration fosters two problems in the media: hypercommercialism and the denigration of public service (McChesney and Nichols 2002, p. 52). As McChesney and Nichols (ibid., p. 55) state:

Nowhere is the commercial marination of the American mind more apparent than in the case of children, where the advertising assault has increased exponentially in the 1990s. ... This desire to indoctrinate fuels the commercial drive into education and suggests that the moral foundations for coming generations may be resting on a dubious base. Nobody knows what the exact consequence of this commercial blitzkrieg upon children will be, but the range of debate extends from 'pretty bad' to 'absolutely terrible.' The only thing we know for certain is that the media giants and advertisers who prosper from it do not care and cannot care. It is outside their frame of reference.

Thus, the basic lesson to be remembered in the political economy of digital literacy is that the primary objective of the media corporations and the entertainment industry is to make a profit, and not to foster democratic thinking or public understanding. The latter is our and our fellow citizens' global task as human beings, social actors and media activists. Vandana Shiva (2003), one of the leading figures of the global democracy movement, writes:

> We are witnessing the worst expressions of organized violence of humanity against humanity because we are witnessing the wiping out of philosophies of inclusion, compassion and solidarity. This is the highest cost of globalization – it is destroying our very capacity to be human. Rediscovering our humanity is the highest imperative to resist and reverse this inhuman project. The debate on globalization is not about the market or the economy. It is about remembering our common humanity. And the danger of forgetting the meaning of being human.

This means that in order to be able to live a democratic life, digital literacy in its various forms is a fundamental prerequisite. In a political economy context, digital literacy is crucial 'to our ability to act as critical, reasoning beings, making judgments about the factors that affect our daily lives' (Wilkin 2002, p. 59). Thus we would like to envision – largely in the spirit of the declaration above – that in the near future the primary educational as well as political meaning of digital literacy has to refer to a world in which everyone has an opportunity to create, access, share and disseminate information and knowledge free of charge in order to educate and empower themselves, and define their quality of life locally and in their own terms. This task, of course, is a contested one, and contradicts the official – yet illusory – world-scale politics of economic agencies, such as the WTO.

One of the most obvious examples of how the WTO policies are further polarising the information societies to come is the TRIPS (trade-related aspects of intellectual property rights) agreement that 'was the first stage in the global recognition of an investment morality that sees knowledge as a private, rather than public, good' (Drahos and Braithwaite 2002, p. 10). The agreement 'effectively globalizes the set of intellectual property principles it contains, because most states of the world are members of, or are seeking membership of, the WTO. ... Every member, for example, has to have a copyright law that protects computer programs as literary works, as well as a patent law that does not exclude micro-organisms and microbiological processes from patentability' (ibid.). Consequently, 'no one disagrees that TRIPS has conferred massive benefits on the US economy ... or that it has strengthened the hand of those corporations with large intellectual property portfolios' (ibid., p. 11).

The problem here is two-fold. First, there is the basic ethico-political problem that knowledge and information that have been created by the many during centuries if not millennia are now, in the twenty-first century, closed and commodified, given to the few. Second, there is the practical problem that an agreement like the TRIPS treaty structurally tends to favour established mega-companies, not the 'copyright-holders' of, say, indigenous knowledge (see Shiva 2001). As for the first, fundamental problem, the UN Economic and Social Council Sub-Comission on Human Rights suggested in August 2000 that implementing the TRIPS agreement may violate basic human rights, including 'the right of everyone to enjoy the benefits of scientific progress and its applications ... there are apparent conflicts between the intellectual property rights regime embodied in the TRIPS agreement, on the one hand, and international human rights law, on the other' (quoted in Drahos and Braithwaite 2002, p. 200).

In sum, an outline of the core ideas of the political economy approach related to the various forms and practices of digital literacy can be presented as follows. First, social phenomena such as digitalisation are located and exist within an historical and structural context shaped by the mode of production and class relations, which change over time. Second, these phenomena of digitalisation should always be analysed in the global context, for they have global effects. Third, different classes and groups have different interests in a digital world, which are often contradictory and conflicting. Fourth, besides the global level the conflicts in the digital world are reflected at the state level, and hence national and regional public policies (that is, EU policies) should be analysed in terms of the varying forms and conditions of inequalities in society (Rantala and Suoranta 2008). Fifth, intellectual and cultural life is formed by the capitalist mode of production, and the struggle for ideological hegemony must happen both in the globalities of the Net and the Wikiworld, and in the institutions of the state and in the civil society. And sixth, we need to emphasise, as Youngman (2000, p. 30) does, that 'opposition to the existing capitalist socioeconomic order is expressed not only by political parties but also by social movements and other organizations in civil society which articulate alternative conceptions of society and how it should develop'. In addition, it is very necessary to maintain that at the present stage of digital literacies many organisations of civil society 'seek to transform people's understanding of society and thereby engage their support in struggles to change society' (ibid., p. 30). The message we take is that the ideological game is not over. It is only starting.

Strong Digital Literacy: The Leap to Authorship

Digital technology creates cultural spaces – such as the Internet – in which the participants are not designated clear-cut roles as 'senders' or 'receivers'. 'Interaction' is the key word of the digital age. Digital technology is different from previous media precisely in that it makes it possible to take part in shaping the 'how' (the vehicle carrying the message) of the storytelling as well as the 'what' (the content of the message) of the story itself. Even if these two could be separated on the abstract level, in practice they work together; the total effect of the story is in the combination. Therefore the analysis of media should also bring the 'what' and the 'how' ultimately together. This need for unity is only increased by the digitalisation of communication technologies.

If digital literacy is considered only from the point of view of skills of interpretation and strategies of reception, the digital media are degraded into just another channel of distribution. This weak or narrow interpretation of digital literacy has to be augmented by a stronger version that includes as its core element a leap to authorship. The concept of authorship in digital literacy refers to the idea of actual freedom as distinct from formal freedom. Paradigmatic examples of formal freedom (and political socialisation) would be choosing from the preset electoral candidates or ready-made curricula or from the pre-existing matrix of proprietary software. On the other hand, actual freedom and actual learning would mean learning from experiences in the context of everyday life in order to transform and change it (for instance, creating revolutionary uses of the Net for local empowerment or using and creating software according to particular needs). In this the terms 'freedom', 'learning' and 'revolution' can be defined, using Ian Parker's (2007, p. 148) words, as 'an opportunity for discovering new ways of living, of bringing to the fore aspects of human creativity and hope that are usually suppressed'.

An essentially Western assumption is, and has been for several decades, that the learning and teaching of diverse modes of literacy belongs to the school. As many thinkers and commentators across the political spectrum and from various disciplines have suggested, this assumption does not necessarily hold any more, for the schooling system, as we know it, is a modern institution which cannot meet the needs and demands of strong digital literacy, and the actualities of everyday life. As Stanley Aronowitz (2004) has pointed out, fiscal exigency and a changing mission have left public education in the US and elsewhere in a chronic state of crisis. Among the main issues is the question of whether schools are failing to transmit the general intellectual culture, its democratic institutions 'and the citizens who are, in the final analysis, responsible for maintaining them'. Aronowitz refers to the words of Hannah Arendt (1961) who went 'so far as to ask whether we "love the world" and our children enough to devise an educational system capable of transmitting to them the salient cultural traditions'.

The leap towards digital authorship prompts an analysis of questions of political economy from a fresh angle. The possibilities of strong digital literacy are not only affected by ownership of channels of distribution or by the impact of social class on education, but also by the self-organising and self-determining creation of communities of communication. In the digital era, the creation of communities implies questions of the ownership of the 'code' which is more like an abstract form than a material quantity. Digital code can be reprogrammed and redistributed, unlike physical objects. The malleability of code, and the 'softness' of software, has given a reason for hoping that digital media is in some sense more democratic than the previous forms of communication. The freedom to create discussion groups, newsletters, global communities, Web logs, and so on, has been seen as a sign of a new renaissance of creativity and resistance in terms of democratic civil society. As the eminent peace researcher Johan Galtung has observed, the trend of media concentration has been counteracted by the Internet revolution. According to Galtung's (2003) optimistic view:

> The access monopoly is to some extent broken. Even a poor village, with neither electricity nor telephone, may sustain one computer powered by solar cells, and connect with a cellular phone if the signal is good enough. They can download technologies produced by intellectuals who have not sold their souls in those Faustian deals with State and Capital. And they may make inputs themselves to the WGIP, the World Gross Idea Product. Sooner or later this will have a revolutionary effect, particularly on the position of the intelligentsia. The world's libraries are available and search engines do the search, which means people not educated/brain-washed by established institutions may see new connections, or prefer to work on the basis of immediate, less mediated experience. The sky is the limit.

Indeed, digital technology has provided new counter-media to the prevalent corporate media. In March 2003, after the attack on Iraq, 'Al Jazeera' replaced 'sex' as the most sought-after term on the Lycos search engine ('Al-Jazeera Site Clicks with Net Users', CBS News 2003; 'Web Surfers Flock to Al-Jazeera' *Wired* 2003). This indicates at least two things. First, the Net is possibly more pluralistic than a corporate TV or newspaper media. Second, it means that people in the North can be moved culturally, socially, and politically by information that contradicts some of their cultural assumptions. In this sense they are capable of being challenged – of being touched, and influenced – and in that sense 'wounded' by content that does not reinforce their presuppositions of the world. While the Qatarian Al Jazeera might not be that far from a cultural setting more familiar to us, it proceeds from concerns and cares which are somewhat different from those of the Western corporate media, and can therefore, at best, throw new light on cultural perceptions and manufactured consent. In a more cynical, or perhaps realistic, sense, one can imagine that there is a constant (information) war in the media sphere, and as a consequence, all the possible means of propaganda and 'perception management' are in active use in the fight between the West and the rest of the world.

However, in the era of digital hegemony and an endless 'war on terror', the idea of digital freedom is more a suggestion to which it is easy to pay lip service than a realistic option. As digitalisation is driven by the push for commercialisation as opposed to the pull of cultural pluralism, there are few signs in the apparently free markets of digitalisation that would benefit the poorest of the poor. Those critical minds living and sharing the everyday traumas of capitalism in developing countries, such as the Indian writer Arundhati Roy, see the present predatory globalisation as a war launched by the rich against the poor in which poverty and protesting against further impoverishment are 'being slyly conflated with terrorism' (Roy 2004). As Roy (ibid.) puts it:

> It goes without saying that every war Empire wages becomes a Just War. This, in large part, is due to the role of the corporate media. It's important to understand that the corporate media doesn't just support the neo-liberal project. This is not a moral position it has chosen to take, it's structural. It's intrinsic to the economics of how the mass media works.

The leap to authorship and the possibility of being touched by information and communication over cultural barriers are indispensable in overcoming the digital hegemony of the Western media giants. Authorship and 'the ethics of being wounded' are among the key factors of strong digital literacy. This pluralist view of the information age implies that we should not think of 'information societies' in the singular with a linear uniform transformation from the industrial era to an informational age and beyond. On the one hand, pluralism and non-linearity mean that the wealthy people of the West are able to be and should be wounded by digitally transported messages and contents from other parts of the world, and, on the other hand, that non-Westerners as 'significant others' are free to find ways of authoring their own digital contents.

Digital Contents as Resources

Digitality as a property of information processing is created by different technological means (electrical, optical, magnetical, and so on), but has the general characteristic of making possible the (near) perfect copying and (near) unlimited distribution of information content. Digital information is essentially binary, consisting of, for example, ones and zeros coded in a suitable physical medium. The reproduction, copying and distribution of digital information (strings of ones and zeros) are substantially different from the reproduction, copying and distribution of analogue information (such as the printed page or speech). The crucial point is that not only is the copying and redistribution of digital information much more precise but digital information can also be copied and redistributed at minimal price compared to analogue information.

As Wilkin (2002, p. 59) has maintained, 'in order for citizens to be able to develop their ideas about politics, economy and culture, it is necessary that there is an adequate supply of information that is both diverse and which aims to inform and challenge received opinions'. But this is not enough. There also have to be adequate means and technologies for the production, distribution, reception and storage of the relevant information. One of the technological beauties of the Internet is that the network is an effective multipurpose distributor of information packets. The

Net does not discriminate between packets on the basis of their content (in fact, the TCP/IP (Transmission Control Protocol/ Internet Protocol) does not provide a way of knowing what the content is).

This basic technological fact has wide socio-political consequences. The most pertinent implication in terms of the political economy of digital literacy is, first, the near-to-zero price of copying and, second, the nearly perfect quality of copies which makes digital content possible as a free public resource. This means that digitalisation has democratic potential: it can act as a scarcity-remover. Once adequate infrastructure is in place, digital information can be made available for everyone at low cost. However, this technological potential is far from reality at the moment. Since the business model of large content-producing corporations (Hollywood's entertainment industry, the software industry, the news and entertainment industry) is based on the scarcity of content, and since digital information and communication technologies (ICTs) have the potential to end that scarcity, it is in the interests of the corporate world to try to create mechanisms of 'artificial' scarcity, and to erect barriers to the abundance of digital content. These mechanisms include legislation ('intellectual property'), technology, policy and education. Digital technology is reducing scarcity, legislation is producing it: this is one of the basic tensions built into information societies.

Even if digital information can remove major barriers to distribution, there is no guarantee that it would actually do so. On the contrary, there is every reason to believe that relative wealth rules the Internet. The notion of 'intellectual property' functions largely as a scarcity-producer. Most assets on intellectual property rights are owned by a few mega-companies from the Northern hemisphere. The idea of intellectual property rights is to commodify content by creating both the legal and technological means, and, more importantly, the ideological will to treat digital content as a commodity, with the ensuing benefits of protection that property enjoys. Given the current forms of economic production and corporate markets, it is important to notice that the liberating potential of digital information necessitates counter-measures that manifest not only in media ownership, but also in policy, legislation and the development of technology. The details of the technological infrastructure both on the hardware and the software side have wide consequences for possibilities of use. And again, what matters is not only the architectural details *per se*, but even more importantly the questions of ownership of technological means (patents, and so on) as well as digital content (copyrights, and so on). The digital technologies that liberate information are the very same technologies that make it possible to have almost perfect control over the distribution of content. A systemic tension between civil societies and the corporate world occurs again and again since the possibility of liberating content applies to copyrighted content too, and because in the digital age the extension of copyright has grown almost exponentially.

The profusion of digital technology contains a mixed if not contradictory set of practices that both support and undermine the development of widespread digital literacy. The basic contradiction is as follows: the rapid development and distribution of digital technology promises to deliver digital information to any place at any time. This is the great democratic potential of digital technology. However, the structure of production and the corporate logic are based on a market where digital content (like any other 'consumer good') is considered as a scarcity and in which its distribution can be controlled so that a continuous revenue stream can be guaranteed. Both an authoritarian national regime and a mega-company like Disney or Microsoft want to control access to information; the former for reasons of controlling political opinion, the latter for reasons of continued demand for commodified information and profit. For both, however, the need for control of digital information creates a need for control of digital technology and, *a fortiori*, of the skills and abilities needed for digital creation. This explains the emphasis on computer and media literacy in the national curricula across the globe and gives a new urgency to the call for strong digital literacy.

3
RADICAL MONOPOLIES

The wish to control digital information implies a need to control and monopolise digital literacy. According to Ivan Illich (1980, p. 55) monopoly has traditionally meant 'exclusive control by one corporation over the means of producing (or selling) a commodity or service'. Radical monopoly, on the other hand, means 'the dominance of one type of product rather than the dominance of one brand'. In other words, monopoly is radical when 'one industrial production process exercises an exclusive control over the satisfaction of a pressing need, and excludes non-industrial activities from competition'. Illich's (ibid., p. 56) example is the school institution which has tried to extend the idea and practice of a radical monopoly on learning by redefining learning as education and training.

One important yet problematic aspect of radical monopoly has been the rise of an expert- and corporate-led society through modern schooling systems. Thus, radical monopoly has existed where learning defined as school education has ruled out natural competence. In addition, the transformation of learning into education paralyses human beings' 'poetic ability', that is, their power to endow the world with personal and socially rewarding meaning. 'Radical monopoly imposes compulsory consumption and thereby restricts personal autonomy. It constitutes a special kind of social control because it is enforced by means of the imposed consumption of a standard product that only large institutions can provide' (ibid.). Radical monopolies have been exercised by mega-corporations that train obedient workers.

Illich (ibid., p. 58) maintains that people have a natural capacity for practices like healing, learning, building their homes, and burying their dead. Each capacity meets a need, and the means for satisfying these needs are abundant 'as long as they depend primarily on what people can do for themselves, with only marginal dependence on commodities'.' In other words, these activities have locally relevant use value instead of abstract exchange value.

The crucial turning point is the moment when these basic capacities can no longer be met by abundant competences; in such a situation peoples' basic satisfactions become scarce. In consequence the establishment of a radical corporate monopoly occurs; people are forced to give up their native ability to do what they could do for themselves and for each other. Radical corporate monopoly thus substitutes standard packages for the personal and social response. It introduces new classes of scarcity (teachers, physicians, information technology technicians, consultants, lawyers, software engineers, and many more experts), and new devices to classify people according to their abilities to act as good consumers. (ibid.) Therefore, radical corporate monopoly makes people dependent on global corporate forces that are not in people's social or political control.

Like literacy in general, digital literacy is rapidly becoming dominated by a radical monopoly in the Western world. Hackers and computer enthusiasts from the 1950s up to the 1970s were able to build their own computers and thus able to satisfy their own ICT needs. While this might still be true for a group of hackers, most people have to learn ICT skills in a world that is almost perfectly controlled by preconfigured computers with monopoly operating systems and web browsers, pre-configured uses of the Internet and the mobile phone. It is this radical monopoly that we need to see as a real threat to strong digital literacy.

The Wikiworld consists of those 'tinkerers' who, in the words of Vaidhyanathan (2004, p. 100), while repairing equipment, 'often master the skills of dubbing, editing, remixing, and distributing video' and other media. However, this kind of 'nativity' in the abilities and mastery of the symbolic forms necessary for the production of digital content is currently being counteracted by a massive trend of commodification of digital information and the architecture of digital technology. This trend concerns not only digital content (such as music, films and stories) but increasingly the very 'code' in which digital content is expressed. The commodification of code happens under the name of 'intellectual property' (IP) – a twentieth-century innovation that spells trouble for the enlightenment ideals of non-authoritarian use of reason and the growth of scientific knowledge. Intellectual property is created through legislation concerning immaterial rights including patents, trademarks and copyrights. During the last century, the term of copyright protection was extended eleven times in the US (Lessig 2001). At the same time, the scope of patentability has grown considerably; in the US concurrently both software (that is, algorithms and their applications) and the biological 'code', such as genes, of organisms can be patented. More importantly, through the actions of institutions such as the World Intellectual Property Organisation (WIPO) and agreements such as TRIPS, the US-style IP legislation has been increasingly globalised. At the same time, through the concentration of ownership of media, software and related companies, the ownership of intellectual property has become increasingly concentrated. It has been estimated that industrial countries hold well over 90 per cent of the world's patents.

The imbalance and inequality of the commodification of IP has been graphically illustrated in the case of bio-patents. Western companies have been able to patent genetic lines of plants, such as rice, which have been in indigenous use for centuries in the developing countries. Such IP schemes clearly create further dependence. However, it often goes unnoticed that when it comes to digital content, the current trend of commodification threatens to create equally big problems of dependence and to create obstacles for digital literacy. If the (software and hardware) tools and skills needed for digital content production are increasingly owned by media and software companies, the possibilities of a globally balanced digital literacy look bleak.

In many developing countries a very high percentage of computer software exists as illegal copies – illegal in terms of the TRIPS-related copyright law. The 'piracy' rates often exceed 90 per cent of the total number of programs in use. When the price of a legal copy of a program often corresponds to several months' if not years' mean income, it is easy to see that the notion of IP effectively functions as a tool for widening the digital divide. Again, there are two issues involved. One concerns the economic side of the issue: the US Congress decided in the nineteenth century not to recognise European 'IP' legislation because paying licence fees to the old continent would have slowed down economic development. It is safe to assume that the emerging global IP regime works in the same way, hindering the economic possibilities of the developing countries.

The other side of the issue has to do with literacy. It is well known that some sort of 'piracy' is often connected to the birth of new ideas and literacies. The Catholic Church did not exactly call the early Protestant translators of the Bible 'pirates', but the content and the tone of the Church's pronouncements was quite close to the content and tone that, for instance, the most rabid proponents of the recording or software industry use in denouncing illegal copying. The historical example also pinpoints the fact that a new kind of literacy is a phenomenon with wide cultural ramifications.

The Pirate Bay

The Pirate Bay is a site for file-sharing using the BitTorrent peer-to-peer network architecture. In a BitTorrent network the files shared are not situated on a central server, but can be retrieved from any of the computers forming the network. Depending on the moment, the network contains a different amount of computers. The Pirate Bay was founded in 2003, and is currently the most popular BitTorrent tracker. The site contains advertisements and the advertising revenue funds the project. Due to the fact that the users sometimes share currently copyrighted material, the Pirate Bay has been repeatedly in trouble with the law. In 2007, the Pirate Bay proposed buying the island Sealand off the British coast in an attempt to form an independent state where copyright would be abolished. As of 2009, several lawsuits are still in progress and plans to sell the site have been published. The future of the site is uncertain, to say the least. (http://thepiratebay.org)

Radical Monopoly and Public Education

Public education is also under threat from multinational corporations that view education as a frontier to be conquered. Critical educators want to fight against the tide of corporate assault and to give teachers and practitioners in formal and non-formal education the necessary tools to fight the capitalist wave. The problem is that more and more education is lacking public funding not only in developing countries but also in those welfare states that are rapidly turning into 'helpfare' states, as in Finland. As Giroux (2003a, p. 471) has put it, the current field of power politics 'appears beyond the reach of governments and as result nations and citizens are increasingly removed as political agents with regards to the impact that multinational corporations have on their daily lives'. Those public places that 'link learning to the conditions necessary for developing democratic forms of political agency and civic struggle' are eliminated.

Manuel Castells (2001, pp. 259–60) has acknowledged the fact that new learning technologies are not used properly in public education. Public education lacks sufficient technological resources, since it is territorially and institutionally differentiated by economic and ethnic factors (class and race). Access to the Internet requires teachers with appropriate proficiencies, but such teachers are unevenly distributed from place to place. In addition, pedagogical climates vary greatly between educational institutions in different countries. In some countries emphasis is put on 'opening the mind' (via experimental curricula, progressive learning and teaching methods, and new information and communication technologies), whereas in other countries, due to a lack of material and human resources, schools are more or less forced to act as child warehouses. Finally, the lack of resources leads to a form of parentocracy in schooling. Parentocracy is a phenomenon in which parents (very often single mothers) have to take responsibility for the totality of their children's upbringing, education and training. In the face of harsh economic and social pressures, the burden can sometimes become too heavy to handle.

In these circumstances, children are bound to learn their 'attested inferiority' (Tammilehto 2003, p. 47).

The general problem of the corporatisation of public education is that, whereas learning is one of the basic human functions both in coping with and in transforming reality, formal education in the modern era has primarily served the aims of the state or capitalism; in the words of Althusser, it has served as a major ideological apparatus. Hence, in the age of digitalisation of information, formal and non-formal education systems in the West have ended up in both internal and financial crises. In order to 'survive', schools, adult education centres and other sites of teaching and learning need to be transformed from 'islands' into 'hearts' at the centre of their own communities, for learning and teaching have always been shared enterprises.

One step towards this transformation is to see formal and non-formal education as phenomena which are tightly integrated into their virtual and 'real' communities. In general terms this integrated view of education consists of two parts (see Suoranta and Lehtimäki 2004, pp. 85–7). The educational foundation would involve learning general skills needed in an information society. However, what constitutes these general skills is a controversial issue: the components that were perceived as general skills before are not necessarily central in today's society. In the end, the notion of general skills is subject to socio-historical context, agreements and values. For example, it may be that, as a result of changes in a nation's values, versatile self-expression is replaced or supplemented by the skill of listening and remaining silent while others speak (see Welton 2002).

With respect to comprehensive education, the following can probably be counted among general skills, the significance of which does not diminish with time and upon which other know-how can be built: reading and writing (understood in the wider sense of digital literacy), counting, and physical and playful cooperation in the form of physical activity that prepares children for sociability and co-ordination. In addition to these general skills, in school education, adult education and higher education, there is a need for integrated multidisciplinary thematic units, which could combine traditional literacy with digital literacy in the use of the various media technologies and versatile and experimental expressive skills. Henry Giroux (2000a, p. 33) writes about experiences in the United States:

> A growing number of alternative school programs and universities have developed very successful media literacy programs and mass communications programs, which, unlike computer technology programs, do not reduce digital literacy simply to learning new skills. These programs allow children and young people to tell their own stories, learn to write scripts, and get involved in community action programs. They also challenge the assumption that popular culture texts cannot be as profoundly important as traditional sources of learning in teaching about important issues framed through, for example, the social lenses of poverty, racial conflict, and gender discrimination.

The integrated view of education should not be based on a short-sighted preparation for the information society. Rather, it should be based on a shift from learning isolated and irrelevant subjects toward a multimodal curriculum that would respond to changes in society, reproducing and challenging the media world as encountered both by children and adults, and through these means enabling the reinforcement of their identities and skills in the art of living as well as the analysis and critique of the global media-cultural situation. If we were to add here the aim of transforming formal and non-formal educational institutions into the nuclei of democratic society, into arenas for participation and oases for caring about other members of the community, we might identify certain values that could foster people's growth into participatory and critical human beings.

We believe that these changes, although necessary but not by any means sufficient, would profoundly affect the way we see and define not only information and teaching as transmitting information, but also the idea of being human in general. These changes in the ideas of formal and non-formal education are part of a struggle against the machine, that is, against the recent trend of superstates like the US and the EU to turn educational institutions (from primary schools to universities) into pure profit-making factories and radical monopolies of information.

Radical Monopoly and Computer Software

Another example of radical monopoly at work is the history of computer software. A classic question concerning literacy has been the question of the access to information using one's native language. The question easily translates to questions of, for instance, the language in which information on the web is presented or the localisation of computer software. Again, the loop should be widened to include questions that have to do with the ability to produce digital content (for example, web content, software, images, video and sound). These abilities are closely related to skills that have to do with the use of the computer and other digital devices; these skills crystallise in their most basic and most powerful form in the skill of programming.

A computer program is typically owned by its author. The end user is given permission to run the program if he or she accepts a licence agreement. The licence agreement states, among other things that the user is not allowed to copy, modify or redistribute the program. Such an act would be technologically possible, even easy (especially if the program was not made technologically more cumbersome by copy-protection measures), but is limited by legislation. This in itself is already an artificially produced loss to the possibilities of strong digital literacy, as well as to the promotion of civil society through digital technology.

The problem, however, runs deeper. The user receives the program in a binary format that the computer can run but which is unintelligible to humans. A person or a programmer would need the source code (written in a programming language, not in ones and zeros) of the program in order to study, understand and eventually modify or produce new versions of the program. Distributing software in closed binary code and bound by strict end user licences is like distributing books in an unreadable, format which cannot be lent to a friend. The proprietary closed-source model for software distribution discourages digital literacy, and in this case the skill of programming. Indeed, it can be claimed that even in the affluent countries the skills needed for digital authorship have not received the attention they require. Digital literacy has been downgraded from the skill of programming to the skill of using Microsoft Windows.

Computer software is a telling example because it is always encoded digitally. Because it is possible to distribute it widely, the measures needed to create artificial scarcity are correspondingly severe. The measures include legislation concerning intellectual property rights (patents, trademarks, copyrights), copy-protection technology, patents on document formats and patents on hardware. The radical monopolisation of the desktop computer space is also a way of creating scarcity and discouraging openness.

The case of software is closely analogous to scientific knowledge (including theories represented in formal code, such as mathematics, large parts of natural science, programming, and so on), which receives its special status and credibility from the very fact that it is not owned: knowledge becomes scientific only through the open and free critique of the scientific community. To quote Jacques Derrida: 'in a scientific text ... the value of the utterance is separated, or cuts itself off, from the name of the author without essential risk, and, indeed, must be able to do so in order to lay claim to objectivity' (Derrida 2002, p. 47). As a speech act, a scientific text has to be distinguished from the person or persons who 'sign' it, otherwise we are not dealing with a text that can assume the special characteristics, and authority of a scientific text. This has been and still is largely the way in which scientific information and knowledge are differentiated from a concept of private property that is dependent on the link between a person and an entity. The author, the one who 'signs' science, is the scientific community. A particular way of speaking, a particular type of speech act, that is, scientific texts, creates a community and a way of appropriating knowledge that is different from the case of private property (as understood, for example, in the Lockean sense).

A similar device for co-operating without the intrusion of private property has been developed in the case of computer software.

So-called free/open source software is built by a community of share and share alike: the goal is to develop software that the user is free to use, modify and redistribute provided that the same freedoms are transferred. In this sense the ideal is close to the ideal of science. For this purpose the movement needs a legal and social tool, one that uses the copyright claim set on a piece of software for community building rather than private property building. This tool, developed by Richard M. Stallman and his co-workers, is often colloquially called *copyleft*: the copyright statement in question gives the user the right to modify and redistribute (the modified version of) the software provided that the same right is also transferred (see Stallman 2002). The cumulative nature of the 'copyleft' copyright protects the information and knowledge amassed in the software from becoming closed by ownership. The knowledge is appropriated by the community.

Both in science and free software, the goal and the prerequisite is a community of sharing based on a certain set of common values and practices. Both can be seen as ways of acting, as power-structures, that are instrumental in creating an information society that contradicts the trends of seeing everything as code and setting up a system of ownership for code. As such, the practices of these communities also demonstrate that digital information processing (or any other technology) does not force us to accept the commodification of code and the ensuing radical monopolies.

Radical Monopoly and Social Media: The Wikipedia and Freedom

Wiki, from the Hawaiian word for 'fast', is a web technology that enables users to modify existing web pages on the fly, to see the history of these changes and to discuss the contents of the page with other users. The technology is best known for the fast-growing encyclopaedia, Wikipedia.org, but it is used also in many other projects of knowledge creation around the Internet. Wiki pages, or in the following just 'wikis', including different wikipedias, benefit from this technology of fast and easy creation and editing. However, it is only in connection with the hacker-originated culture of freedom on the Net that the wiki technology realises its true potential.

The Wikipedia project has its roots in the hacker movement working in order to provide free software. The ambiguity of the word 'free' merits further attention. The Wikipedia is free in the sense of '*gratis*', but, more importantly, it is free in the sense of 'free speech'. The Wikipedia is licensed under the Gnu Free Documentation License (GFDL) innovated by Richard M. Stallman and the Free Software Foundation. In essence, the licence says that one can use, distribute and modify text licensed under the GFDL provided that the redistributed and modified versions are also licensed under GFDL. This makes GFDL a so-called copyleft licence. It uses copyright law in order to give the users more rights: the rights of redistribution and modification.

A copyleft licence guards the content from lock-in or privatisation: no institution can take the content and commodify it. Ideally, this freedom is for ever. In fact, like free software, free information under the GFDL has no exchange value, but does have a potentially substantial use value. In this sense a combination of wiki technology and of copyleft licensing (such as exists in the case of the Wikipedia and many other wikipedias and wikis) provides a prototype for a new kind of 'knowledge work'. The social and political effects of such production are interesting and debated (see, for example, Hardt and Negri 2004, p. 301ff.; Žižek 2002b, 2006b; Merten 2000). From the perspective of economics, the question of motivation is one of the most crucial: Why do people engage in volunteer work like this without immediate financial rewards? The conditions under which voluntary non-alienated work are possible are of the utmost importance for the critical potential of open collaborative projects like the Wikipedia. We will return to this question after looking more closely at the promise of the Wikipedia.

The Wikipedia has an obvious Gutenbergian potential. It is a free encyclopaedia providing all the emancipatory potential of the encyclopaedias of the Enlightenment era, such as the *Encyclopédie ou dictionnaire raisonné des sciences, des arts et des métiers* (1751–72) by Diderot and D'Alembert. It makes encyclopaedic knowledge accessible for free everywhere where the Internet is available, and in some cases even where it is not. Cd-roms with a stable version of the Wikipedia, and even printed editions and special wikibooks are being produced to overcome the lack of Internet infrastructure. If Gutenberg's revolution was about making printed media more abundant, the Wikipedia has the same effect on digital information but on a different order of magnitude.

The Gutenbergian effect of the Wikipedia with its different language versions is already being felt in educational institutions. Students are known to 'borrow' material from the Wikipedia. Educators relying on the reproduction of ingested material in order to supervise the process of learning are having a hard time fighting this kind of use. More noteworthy is the fact that many teachers from the primary to the tertiary levels are starting to feel that some subjects that until now have been taught using traditional lectures (like 3D animation engines, TCP/IP protocol and other 'nerdy' subjects where the current state of the Wikipedia is most advanced) are better presented in the Wikipedia, and that their energies would be better spent elsewhere. This migration from the lecture to the Wikipedia will in future be felt in all subjects in one way or another and will contribute to the changing nature of education and expertise.

However, this Gutenbergian potential is not the most interesting part of the Wikipedia with regard to issues of critical media literacy or pedagogy. The fact that the Wikipedia is free in the sense of free speech, is, in our estimate, going to be much more influential. This second freedom has two important consequences that together can over time completely change our views on things like education, literacy and expert knowledge. Let us call these the 'internal' and the 'external' perspectives: 'internal' meaning the process of creating wikipedia content, and 'external' concentrating on wikipedias as whole entities. We do not want to call these the producers' and users' perspectives, as the point is precisely that the division between these roles will be blurred (Peters and Lankshear 1996, p. 62).

The External Perspective: The Proliferation of Wikipedias

From the external perspective, the 'free speech' freedom of the Wikipedia creates possibilities for limitless forking, that is, new modified versions based on existing ones (for forks of the Wikipedia, see http://en.wikipedia.org/wiki/Wikipedia:Mirrors_ and_forks). We should, indeed, be talking of the class of wikipedias, in which the current Wikipedia with its various language versions is one case and wikipedias – such as the Conservapedia (http:// www.conservapedia.org), 'The Conservative Wikipedia' – with different viewpoints or attitudes form the next class. In fact, the different language versions can already be classified as content forks, since their content is different to some extent (see, for example, the English and French articles on human reproductive organs). The reasons for forking Wikipedia have so far included editorial policy, attitudes on advertising and, most importantly, different rationalities or points of view behind the content. In essence, when talking about the forks of the Wikipedia or the class of wikipedias in general, we are dealing with the politics of knowledge production.

Currently, the Wikipedia has a policy of 'Neutral Point Of View' (NPOV): while discussing controversial issues, Wikipedia articles 'must represent all significant views fairly and without bias'. The NPOV is self-consciously a view, not the absence of all views. This means that, like the Encyclopaedias of the Enlightenment, the Wikipedia does contain a rationality of its own. The excessively scientific-positivist rationality of the Enlightenment has been amply criticised in the last hundred years or so. We have learned that, far from being a boon to all humanity, as it believed itself to be, Enlightenment rationality meant the suppression, if not worse, of different rationalities and people believing in them. While the Wikipedia's NPOV is not as rabid as the most virulent forms of Enlightenment rationality, it is clear that the growing prominence of Wikipedified information will be corrosive towards certain types of communal, religious and other rationalities. However, the possibility of forking the Wikipedia somewhat mitigates this negative aspect.

Some kind of common rationality is necessary for any kind of open collaborative project to work. In the case of free/open source software, the criteria for an improvement of the code are quite straightforward. If the new code works better, it is better. In the case of the Wikipedia, the NPOV provides the necessary goal-oriented rationality and makes it possible to decide what is an improvement over an existing version of an article. It is clear that the NPOV is not the only possible criterion for improvements. Consequently, different wikipedias with different rationalities are emerging. The development of non-neutral wikipedias goes way beyond the Gutenbergian revolution. Editing Wikipedia articles is easy. Given time, many political, gendered, geographical, ethnic, and so on, viewpoints will have wikipedias of their own. Already a whole universe of different wiki projects exists on the Net, from the sustainability wiki of Finnish eco-villages to the gambling wikis of Las Vegas.

This radical proliferation of non-neutral point of view (nNPOV) wikipedias will provide a wide spectrum for critical literacy. Not only are we able to learn from various points of view, we will also be able to formulate and argue for our own. The radical proliferation not only concerns points of view. The level of difficulty and need for active participation from the reader may be varied at will, as well. Already many Wikipedia articles are formed by providing a combination of short versions of longer articles. This fractal nature of wiki information will also provide an active playground for critical reasoning: sometimes understanding demands more information, sometimes less.

Limitless forking is not a value in itself; the Internet is already full of more or less useless information. However, in the hands of a group of committed individuals and intellectuals working towards a more or less shared goal in incremental steps, wikis provide essential possibilities. Free knowledge production in terms of copyleft does deliver – *mutatis mutandis* – something of Marx's ideas in his 'Critique of the Gotha Program' (1875):

> In a higher phase of communist society, after the enslaving subordination
> of the individual to the division of labour, and therewith also the antithesis

between mental and physical labor, has vanished; after labour has become not only a means of life but life's prime want; after the productive forces have also increased with the all-around development of the individual, and all the springs of co-operative wealth flow more abundantly – only then can the narrow horizon of bourgeois right be crossed in its entirety and society inscribe on its banners: From each according to his ability, to each according to his needs!

The Internal Perspective: Wikis as Ideal Communication

A Wikipedia article comes not only with a button to the edit page, but also with a history and a discussion page. These two provide a unique perspective on how the content has been created, criticised and co-operatively developed. Already the existence of the 'edit' button indicates a subtle but profound epistemological shift: knowledge comes with a past and a future; it is not immutable 'black on white'.

The newspaper as a medium in which argument based on the public use of one's reason – Kant's definition of adulthood and maturity in his 'An Answer to the Question: What is Enlightenment' (1784) – has been particularly celebrated as a cornerstone of democratic discussion and decision making. The newspaper has also been criticised by Kierkegaard and others as levelling down genuine expression. Now that commodified messages and mainstreamed content is taking over even so-called quality newspapers, their role as an open and participatory public discussion forum in the sense of Habermas or Dewey is rapidly declining, and Kierkegaard's worry seems justified.

However, something of the Kantian-Habermasian public space is being recreated in the discussions around Wikipedia content. The NPOV explicitly endorses Habermasian discourse, where the conditions of ideal communication are explicitly upheld by the guidelines of NPOV itself. These discussions have two aspects: the political and the epistemological.

On the epistemological side, the processual nature of wiki content emphasises the pragmatic and public aspects of knowledge, disregarding or circumventing aspects of authorship and credentials. Discussions on the reliability of Wikipedia articles often miss the interesting internal change: the reliability of a Wikipedia article is not (only or mainly) to be examined on the basis of the article as it stands, but also by looking at how it has been developed and what kind of criticism it has withstood. This widely distributed peer review gives wiki content a reliability that is different from that guaranteed by authors with institutional credentials. Currently proposals are being made on how visual cues – for example, colour – could be used in highlighting well-established content on a wiki page (see Cross 2006).

On the political side, the Wikipedia and, even more importantly, other open, collaborative wikis, are currently functioning as hotbeds for democratic discussion and education throughout the world. The nNPOV wikis formed by special interest groups or communities with common problems have perhaps the most to gain as the 'real world' aims and objectives of those involved act as a dynamo for collaborative knowledge creation. With the 'edit', 'history' and 'discuss' buttons, information on a wiki page is obviously a collective process, not an individual's possession. This epistemological shift, together with the proliferation of wikipedias, will have a dramatic effect on education and learning. Community wikis and larger, open wikipedias are already building the public spheres of the future.

Breaking Radical Monopolies: Digital Opportunities and Real Impossibilities

The hope engendered by the emergence of social media like the Wikipedia lies in the promised post-scarcity and non-alienated mode of labour. Even if a cybercommunist utopia is still far away – What will the hackers eat? Will everyone be a hacker? – a change can already be felt inside the hegemonic forms of production. By adopting aspects of the social media, the first economy of commodities and markets – or less euphemistically, capitalism – tries to present itself 'with a human face'. This imitation is felt on many fronts: schools and universities want to expand their scope by providing access to informal learning using social media tools, presenting themselves as hubs of social interaction, rather than as formal institutions of power; nation states want to shift attention from traditional industries to competition in terms of design and cultural capital; and companies invite their customers to co-create their future products in a process in which innovation itself is supposedly dispersed and equalised (for 'innovation' in the new setting, see Thrift 2006).

Again, Žižek (2008, p. 18, quoting Olivier Malnuit 2006) has his finger on the pulse when he discusses a new form of business, in which 'no one has to be vile'. One crucial step removed from the utopia of cybercommunism, Žižek calls this new ideal of frictionless and nomadic capitalism with a human face, 'liberal communism':

1. You shall give everything away free (free access, no copyright); just charge for the additional services, which will make you rich.
2. You shall change the world, not just sell things.
3. You shall be sharing, aware of social responsibility.
4. You shall be creative: focus on design, new technologies and science.
5. You shall tell all: have no secrets, endorse and practise the cult of transparency and the free flow of information; all humanity should collaborate and interact.
6. You shall not work: have no fixed 9 to 5 job, but engage in smart, dynamic, flexible communication.
7. You shall return to school: engage in permanent education.
8. You shall act as an enzyme: work not only for the market, but trigger new forms of social collaboration.
9. You shall die poor: return your wealth to those who need it, since you have more than you can ever spend.
10. You shall be the state: companies should be in partnership with the state.

This is all well and good, as far as it goes. But the liberal communist economy conveniently forgets the essential structural conditions of its own existence. For Bill Gates to give huge sums to charity from his personal fortune, he first had to collect it using ruthless monopolistic practices. More generally,

> Developed countries are constantly 'helping' undeveloped ones (with aid, credits etc.), and so avoiding the key issue: their complicity in and responsibility for the miserable situation of the Third World. [O]utsourcing is the key notion. You export the (necessary) dark side of production – disciplined, hierarchical labor, ecological pollution – to 'non-smart' Third World locations (or invisible ones in the First World). (Žižek 2006b)

What liberal communism hides, deliberately or not, is the structural violence inherent in global capitalism.

Yahoo Answers

Yahoo Answers is a service maintained by the Yahoo Company where people can present precise questions like 'What documents would I need to visit Canada?' or 'What are the advantages of mats over dirt floors in horse stables?' and the answers are provided by registered volunteers. In a familiar web 2.0 fashion, the community of users provides the content for the service and Yahoo profits by displaying advertisements on the site. Yahoo Research Director Marc Davis maintains that the strength of Yahoo Answers derives from the fact that everyone is an expert on something and, with the increased amount of free time on our hands, is also willing to share his or her expertise. In terms of copyrights the approach is ambiguous; Yahoo does not claim any responsibility for the contents and urges users to respect copyright law. (http://answers.yahoo.com/)

Žižek points out that liberal communism can work only by masking the structural (economic, social and political) violence on which its outsourced practices are based. Against this he insists on a true universalism that transcends all local (ethnic, national, gendered, and so on) identities. Local identities are not, for Žižek, a force against global capitalism, as it is only too happy to manipulate, create and commodify such identities. We might ask does not the utopia of liberal communism itself contain a certain amount of structural violence, a violence that is familiar from the earlier stages of cultural change?

Let us proceed according to the hypothesis that the areas designated by the phrase 'creative industries' are precisely the places where the structural bias and consequent violence of the cybercommunist utopias may be discerned. Since the free/open-source software movement is so often presented as the paradigm of the new forms of intellectual labour, let us consider for a moment the crown jewel of that movement, the GNU/Linux operating system. Linux is available free for anyone to use, modify and redistribute on the Net. In 2002, it was estimated that a typical GNU/Linux distribution (Debian) contains more that 55 million lines of source code; if it were to be created using traditional proprietary methods of software development, the cost would be US$1.9 billion (Gonzáles-Barahona et al. 2002). That was in 2002; by now, its value will have grown further. It is easy to see that this kind of value created and distributed freely is indeed new: germs of non-commodity exchange, indeed. The fact that GNU/Linux has tremendous use value for thousands of people around the world shows how freely co-operating and self-organising communities can do real work. The transfer of skills and knowledge happening in the Linux community may be one of the best examples we have of a global volunteer organisation.

Nevertheless, the structures of inequality quickly kick in. Most Linux-kernel developers are male and relatively young. Moreover, most of them come from North America or Europe. In the case of Debian, this holds true. The developers have typically received some academic education, and the number of PhD holders in the group is quite high – over 10 per cent. Again, most of the developers come from the global North (see, for example, Mikkonen et al. 2007). This geopolitical bias is not just an historical fact, a relic created by the initiation of these projects in the North. During the 15 years or so the projects have been in progress, only minor change has occurred, with individual programmers from Brazil, India and some other Southern countries getting involved. Indeed, there is as much reason to believe that the economic divisions in the real world are exacerbated in the digital world as to believe that there are grounds for hoping that digital technology could bridge these divides. If we consider that, from summer 2005 to summer 2006, the Linux kernel received more new code from the .mil domain (US military) than from most Third World countries, we see the old colonialism continuing in new guises.

Or let us go back to the Wikipedia. The English Wikipedia has circa 3 million articles (as of September 2009), and other language versions are developing quickly. The non-neutral neutrality of the NPOV was mentioned, above. If we like the Habermasian communicative rationality, the NPOV is nice, but it is corrosive with regard to certain types of communities. In order for a wikipedia to work, it needs a certain critical mass (to resist vandalism, to promote increased content, diversification of contributor roles, and so on). The smaller the (linguistic) community, or the group with a shared worldview, the lower the chances of a vibrant Wikipedia. Furthermore, critical mass means normalisation, which in itself works against certain types of communal identities. From the user's point of view, the fact that the English Wikipedia is so much better than, say, the Finnish one, provides an additional pull towards the hegemonic language and its values.

These two small examples should serve to indicate that the liberal communist utopia is by no means neutral with regard to local identities. Indeed, we might suspect that the power structures of the first economy are visible in the digital sphere. If this is the case, the drive towards culture as the playground of global commerce reveals a new side. The opportunities for small linguistic areas like Finland to make successful business out of the creative industries look bleak, notwithstanding the digital opportunities. The Sibeliuses and Alvar Aaltos of previous generations learned their trade from Europe and, by cleverly infusing it with 'local' colouring, sold it back to the source. Being a classical composer or being a modern architect are European occupations, and a Finn can succeed in these only insofar as he or she is able to become European. And what else is 'European' than an ideological discursive construction? Why would things be any different with regard to digital creation? Finland, to be sure, is a wealthy, highly modernised nation, with a well-educated population. This is one of the reasons why advanced technology has been one of our success stories. But what, after all, is this 'ours', and 'us', and what is the 'Finnish culture' in, say, Nokia mobile phones? Precious little. Again, even the design of the phones recycles a global style, with minor improvements, and production is outsourced to the point where nobody wants to know about the toxic trail leading to illegal mines in Nigeria. If the promise of 'creative liberal communism' is an empty one, as in the case of Finland, what can it be like in other, equally small, but less prosperous cultural areas?

Corresponding to the demand for stylish mobile phones in the market, there is zero demand for the non-European parts of Finnish culture, such as *eräkirjallisuus* ('wilderness literature'), in which hunting and fishing trips are described in endless variations on the short-story formula. This type of literature is not politically correct, since it involves the killing of animals, is mostly read and written by non-elitist males, and in a ritual way always revolves around the same narrative: leaving home for nature, hunting or fishing, and gaining something in the process. No amount of digital revolution will wash away this political incorrectness and make Finnish wilderness literature desirable for the European or global public. Better to write detective novels – a European genre – with a local flavour; the popularity of Scandinavian detective fiction is a case in point.

All of this points to the fact that, in the case of small cultures and linguistic areas, the problems and possibilities of the digital era are significantly different from those of the bigger, more dominant players. It also means that attempts to understand intellectual labour or the creative industries cannot rely exclusively on the tools created in critical discussions in the heart of Europe. The post-post-isms emerging from Italy or France have only so much purchase in a landscape that is only now entering the phase that cultural critics like Adorno described in their classic postwar writings. In Finland, the first generation that likes to shop, and which has never really worried about spending money and not saving it, is only now emerging. Likewise, a mass public for soap operas is a very recent phenomenon. Consequently, the critical analysis of a mass society and cultural industry is becoming topical at the very moment that it is also being left behind.

If this non-synchronicity is true of such a pseudo-European area as Finland, what can be said of other non-European or non-Westerns places? We strongly suspect that a co-existence of different world-eras – distinct stages of development with different goals and values – around the globe makes it impossible to utilise only the latest theory from Paris or California, as if only the latest would be advanced enough. Indeed, globalisation is reinforcing, for instance, both class distinctions (mobile phone assemblers in Finland and China have more in common with each other than with their compatriot managers) and ethnic identities (as environmental crises threaten local nature). If there are histories of the world that are not the history of Europe, then we also need multiple theories of the information society.

4

THE WORLD DIVIDED IN TWO

We are living in a world of dramatic cultural, economic, social and educational oppositions. These distinctions are largely dependent on whether the person in question was born in the rich North or the poor South. By North and South, we refer to the economic, social and educational gulf prevailing in the world at the moment. In the South, people die of malnutrition, whereas in the North, among the most common causes of death is being overweight. While in the South people are living under the regimes of corrupt governments, in conditions best described as a state of societal chaos, people in the political totalitarianism of the North are discussing the reasons and consequences of the democratic deficit. While in the North the use of the appliances of ICTs is skyrocketing, in the South a significant portion of the population – over 800 million adults, two-thirds of whom are women – still lack basic literacy.

From a very general perspective, peoples' living conditions vary to unimaginable degrees. First, we can't sufficiently stress the fact that people today are growing up in economically, culturally, historically and socially different worlds. However, in contrast to this immense variation, there exists a grand narrative: the unprecedented and unifying educational power of a global media culture, which challenges and often surpasses such traditional forms of socialisation as family and school. As observed by Douglas Kellner (2000, p. 305):

> Culture had been a particularizing, localizing force that distinguished societies and people from each other. Culture provided forms of local identities, practices, and modes of everyday life that could serve as a

bulwark against the invasion of ideas, identities, and forms of life extraneous to the specific local region in question.

At present, however, the status and meaning of culture has changed: 'culture is an especially complex and contested terrain today as global cultures permeate local ones and new configurations emerge that synthesize both poles, providing contradictory forces of colonization and resistance, global homogenization and new local hybrid forms and identities' (ibid.). In literature, this complex cultural situation, where people are forced to struggle for their lives, living conditions and identities, has been given a variety of names. Some call it the 'information' or 'informational age', others term it 'technoculture' (Robins and Webster 1999) or 'techno-capitalism', 'global media culture' or simply 'globalisation', referring to the dialectical process in which the global and the local exist as 'combined and mutually implicating principles' (Beck 2002, p. 17). A number of other labels, such as 'post-industrial', 'virtual' or 'cybersociety', are also used (see Hand and Sandywell 2002), but the notion behind these descriptions is that, across the globe, ICTs are playing a central role in people's lives, as well as in society at large.

The first assumption behind these terms is that the proliferation of ICTs is causing a rapid transformation in all branches of life. The second underlying idea is that ICTs function to unify and standardise culture. A variety of grand narratives have been produced on the topic of media culture. Manuel Castells (2001, p. 2) analyses some of the imperatives that have characterised the transformation from the industrial to the informational era:

> The needs of the economy for management flexibility and for the globalization of capital, production, and trade; the demands of society in which the values of individual freedom and open communication became paramount; and the extraordinary advances in computing and telecommunications made possible by the micro-electronics revolution.

The grand narratives of contemporary society are rarely told from the standpoint of the ordinary citizen, not to mention children and young people especially in the developing countries.

The processes behind terms like 'global media culture' deserve a more thorough analysis from the point of view of ordinary lifeworlds. The same can be said of media culture in its entirety: it is largely affected and infected by Western values ignorant of other worldviews and cultures. When talking about bridging the digital divide, it is thus important to recall that ICTs carry a number of Western values – a cultural package, so to speak – not directly transferable to other cultures. The media culture comprises both traditional media, including print media, television and the telephone, and the more recent ICTs, such as computers, the Internet and mobile phones. All of these appliances are saturated with Western popular culture and advertising.

Typically, the debate about the meaning of ICTs moves between two polarities: utopias and dystopias. Pessimists and cynics who believe that the core meaning of ICTs is one of cultural barbarism challenge technology enthusiasts who believe that ICTs will revolutionise every aspect of the world. Somewhere in between there are those who collect statistics about the global diffusion of ICTs with little emphasis on their interpretation. The latter group often forgets that statistical reasoning is a value-laden interpretive act in itself. Furthermore, the media itself is keen to inform the public but lacks the critical capacity to evaluate the core meaning of ICTs (Castells 2001, p. 3). Those more or less autonomous researchers who are doing their best to gain a better understanding of the current situation provide another vantage point. Unfortunately, critical and analytical thinkers with the capacity and willingness to put forward ideas that go beyond technological determinism are few in number.

Our perspective is two-fold. First, we fully appreciate the fact that ICTs represent a Western value package, but it is also our understanding that people are capable of interpreting and using ICTs in diverse and novel ways, thus investing them with their own meanings. Second, we have deep misgivings about the technological determinism evident in many discourses on ICTs. Technological determinism fosters assumptions about ICTs having the power to overcome the current maladies of the world including poverty, hunger and deprivation and the conflicts arising from them. Our stance on the issue could be described as critical yet cautiously hopeful and optimistic, the main question being, what are the terms on which this optimism can be sustained in the age of technological cynicism?

Global Media and Information Culture

The discussion on media culture and the information society contains powerful simplifications as it operates on exaggerations and often has very little to do with reality as experienced by young people. A wide range of definitions and characterisations has sprung up around global media and information culture. Generally, the concept 'media culture' refers to the socio-cultural condition in which most young people's daily perceptions and experiences are indirect and transmitted through various ICTs, whether traditional (radio, television and newspaper) or new (mobile phone, computer). Some of the definitions of media culture emphasise the significance of information *per se* and the information technology that has emerged around it. Manuel Castells' *magnum opus*, *The Information Age* (Castells 1996), is a paramount example of this emphasis. Castells' account of the network society, the economic and social dynamics of the new informational age, is strongly reminiscent of the analysis once conducted by Marx on the industrial society. The most fundamental difference between the two is that, where Marx emphasised industrial labour as the basis for all productivity, Castells (ibid., p. 17) stresses the meaning of information and information flows:

> In the industrial mode of development, the main source of productivity lies in the introduction of new energy sources, and in the ability to decentralize the use of energy throughout the production and circulation processes. In the new informational mode of development, the source of productivity lies in the technology of knowledge generation, information processing, and symbol communication.

In the footsteps of Marshall McLuhan, Castells (2001) has further argued that the Internet is the defining symbol of our times; that it is the medium that forms the fabric of our very lives. For Castells, the network represents the leading idea of our era and functions as a metaphor extending its influence to various aspects of human activity: 'Core economic, social, political, and cultural activities throughout the planet are being structured by and around the Internet, and other computer networks', he contends (ibid., p. 3): 'Exclusion from these networks is one of the most damaging forms of exclusion in our economy and in our society.' He then goes on to compare the meaning of information technology with that of electricity in the industrial era, likening the Internet to the electrical grid or the electric engine: the Internet can distribute the power of information throughout the entire realm of human activity.

The central position of information also dictates the type of competencies required from a labour force in the future. Perhaps the most central capabilities are those of learning and re-learning and managing information. Castells' writings on the matter are far from one-dimensional: he acknowledges the versatile and contradictory character of the global media and information culture. For instance, that ICTs can be used both as the accelerator of immaterial flows of value, such as money and free trade, and as the information channel for various social movements and anti-corporate activism. The foundation of Castells' analysis as well as its conception of the essence of the information society rests on economic activity. In fact, the term 'information economy' is exactly right for the model of society constructed in Castells' theories. More than technological determinism, Castells' thinking seems to be guided and motivated by the ICT imperative. The following quote from Hand and Sandywell (2002, p. 198) illustrates this type of thinking well: 'Where information technologies have been singled out as key causes of progressive change and democratic enlightenment, we not only have an instance of ideological simpli-fication but also an advanced form of technological fetishism.'

Where Castells and his kind emphasise access to information as a factor in global and macroeconomic success, other people (for example, Kellner 1995; Webster 2000; Norris 2001; May 2001) highlight the importance of surrounding cultural, political and social factors in the construction of the global media and information culture. In short, they believe that the lifeworld should involve something more than just ICTs. Only after a thorough analysis of these factors surrounding ICTs can we say something about the significance of the global media culture in general and ICTs in particular. From a sociological viewpoint, global media culture has often been associated with the substitution of the national by the global: 'the logic of manufacturing is displaced by the logic of information; and the logic of the social is displaced by that of the cultural' (Lash 2002, p. 26). The sovereignty of nation states – the economic, political and cultural relationships between independent states – is being replaced by global flows such as finance, technology, information, communication, images, ideas or people. The logic of manufacturing is giving way to the logic of information. This means that a vast array of products is becoming more informationalised: for example, toys and computer games are becoming increasingly digitalised. Moreover, work and production processes are no longer labour-intensive, but information-, knowledge- and design-intensive. Furthermore, the social is being displaced by the cultural: where the social was tied to place and tradition, in the world of wired connections, the cultural flows as freely as money, ideas and popular images (ibid.).

In his largely sceptical take on the information society, Christopher May (2001, pp. 12–17) has located four central, yet problematic, claims about current media culture. The first claim is that, above all, the meaning of media culture is that of a social revolution induced by the manifestations of information technology, such as computers, mobile phones and the Internet. As observed by May, the claim represents technological determinism and forgets that the meaning of technology is not to be found in technology itself, but arises from its usages and the cultural-political context. He goes on to contend that (ibid., p. 14), 'Once we recognize that there has been a long gestation of the relevant technologies and of their interaction with societies across the globe, then the claims for revolution start to look a little strained.'

The second claim foresees a replacement of the rigid social, political and judicial institutions by an ICT-based new economy and a Californian ideology. The global development of Californi-sation is about autonomous individuals who communicate with other autonomous individuals with the primary aim of finding new ways to make money. The new economy offers no hope for longstanding or permanent jobs that would create stability and social security in young people's lives. In the weightless economy of the future, young people in the North work primarily in flexible, part-time, half-pay service sector jobs, while the youth of the South slave away in sweatshops. The third claim suggests that, in the pre-Internet world, many writers stressed the significance of expert power afforded by management, control, ownership and distribution of information. The age of the Internet has witnessed the spread of what one might call a do-it-yourself ideology. Its central assumption is that people automatically mobilise into small and efficient interest groups and social movements and no longer require traditional parties or social institutions to achieve their aims.

The final claim is that nation states and national educational policies are slowly disappearing from the political scene. According to this view, 'the information revolution has undermined the state's ability to control information for its own ends, with fatal consequences for its overall authority' (ibid., p. 16). Of course, the claim is exaggerated, as in many senses nation states and national educational policies remain powerful categories in global politics and there are no signs of their disappearance.

In the same tone, Zygmunt Bauman (1998, p. 53) has his say on the revolutionary possibilities of the Internet – written before the birth of social media:

> Contrary to what academics, themselves members of the new global elite, tend to believe, the Internet and Web are not for anyone and unlikely ever to become open to universal use. Even those who get access are allowed to make their choices within the frame set by the suppliers, who invite them 'to spend time and money choosing between and in the numerous packages they offer'. As for the rest, left with the network of satellite or cable television with not as much as a pretention to symmetry between the two sides of the screen – pure and unalloyed watching is their lot.

The Media Culture

It is unnecessary to labour the point that the majority of the content of current media culture is of Western origin and is produced mainly in the US by Hollywood's entertainment industry. Its contents are blind to people's – defined as consumers – cultural, economic and educational backgrounds, as well as their social status. The logic of Western media culture is largely based on the old model of broadcasting: from the few mastodons of communication to the many. The same is true of large portions of the Internet, despite the fact that it has been hailed as a subversive instrument, thanks to its potential for many-to-many communication. Prevailing media culture is, at least to some extent, culturally blind and ruled by a small number of media giants. The concept of media culture refers to an increase in different mediated signs and messages and a play of interlacing meanings. The media saturated by popular culture penetrates such fields of reality as politics, economy, free time and education. At present, global media culture is a pedagogic force that has the power to far exceed the achievements of institution-alised forms of education. As Giroux (2000a, p. 32) puts it:

> With the rise of new media technologies and the global reach of the highly concentrated culture industries, the scope and impact of the educational force of culture in shaping and refiguring all aspects of daily life appear unprecedented. Yet the current debates have generally ignored the powerful pedagogical influence of popular culture, along with the implications it has for shaping curricula, questioning notions of high-status knowledge, and redefining the relationship between the culture of schooling and the cultures of everyday life.

However, the concept of media culture does not refer simply to symbolic combinations of immaterial signs or capricious currents of new and old meanings, but to an entire way of life (see Lash 2002, p. 13), where images, signs, texts and other audio-visual representations are connected with the real fabric of material realities, symbols and artificialities (see also Giroux 2000a, p. 98). Media culture is pervasive: its messages are an important part of the everyday lives of people and their daily activities are structured around media use. The stories and images in the media become important tools for identity construction. Film stars, musicians and other celebrities endorse commodities and stimulate demand, while the language used by a cartoon character becomes an important factor in the street-credibility of young people. In the present situation, few corners of the world have escaped the meanings embedded in televised media culture.

In a mediated culture, it can be difficult for young people to know whose representations are closest to the truth, which representations to believe and whose images matter. This is partly because the emergence of digitalised communication and the commoditisation of culture have significantly altered the conditions of experiencing life and culture. Many people perhaps still feel attached to the romantic image of the old organic communities, where people would converse with each other face to face and live in a close-knit local environment. Digital communication, however, is gradually eliminating the romantic image:

> Most of the ways in which we make meanings, most of our communications to other people, are not directly human and expressive, but interactions in one way or another worked through commodities and commodity relations: TV, radio, film, magazines, music, commercial dance, style, fashion, commercial leisure venues. These are major realignments. (Willis 2000, p. 48)

Media culture is produced and reproduced by diverse ICTs. Thus it is imperative to replace the teaching and training of the knowledge and skills needed in the agrarian and industrial societies with education in digital literacy, or, as Colin Lankshear and Michele Knobel have suggested, in digital *literacies*:

> Approaching digital literacy from the standpoint of digital *literacies* can open us up to making potentially illuminating connections between literacy, learning, meaning (semantic as well as existential), and experiences of agency, efficacy, and pleasure that we might not otherwise make. The point here is not simply to import an array of digital literacies holus bolus into classroom on the grounds that they are 'engaging,' or because learners who do not experience success in conventional school subject literacies can

nonetheless experience success and affirmation as bloggers, gamers and fan practice aficionados – although that would be no small thing. Rather, the educational grounds for acknowledging the nature and diversity of digital literacies, and for considering where and how they might enter into *educational* learning have partly to do with the extent to which we can build bridges between learners' existing interests in these practices and more formal scholarly purposes. (Lankshear and Knobel 2008, p. 9)

A similar point is made by Kellner (1998a, p. 122), who contends that in a media culture it is important to learn multiple ways of interacting with social reality. Students must be provided with opportunities to develop skills in multiple literacies, in order for them to be able to work on their identities, social relationships and communities, whether material, virtual or combinations of the two.

The ICT Debate

The ICT debate has many levels and layers. From a technological-administrative perspective the main issues involve Internet diffusion, access to the Internet and use skills. The discussion is seemingly value neutral. Nonetheless, a belief in progress, technology and the market economy is evident in this discourse. As can be expected, enabling access to the Internet constitutes a key issue for the players in global economy. The opportunity to use the Internet is also a central issue in welfare politics promoting equal opportunities for young people. Aside from concerns related to market value and equal opportunities, an important criticism concentrates on the digital divide, which is perceived as distinct from more elementary worldwide problems (cf. Castells 2001, p. 269). Another perspective emphasises the social structures of the Internet and the inequalities surrounding it. The emphasis is on social problems that emerge as by-products of the Internet culture.

The adoption and use of technologies is believed to reflect and aggravate social inequalities, but also to increase the rate of employment and build up the information technological infrastructure required by social justice. The consequences of ICT use and solutions are still largely unknown in terms of social inequalities and employment although one thing is sure. There is no ready-made model of ICT use for everyone. Different cultural contexts need different solutions, and different solutions lead to different results.

Yet another concern is that of the digital divide between the information-rich and the information-poor; it demonstrates a belief in traditional political intervention in which national educational and social policies and legislation are formed to narrow the emerging gaps. Thus political decision-making and independent scientific research and development hold a key position when tackling the economic and social problems of information societies and especially the problem of the digital divide, which in many texts is seen as a grave structural problem. The discourse of the information-rich and the information-poor advocates welfare state politics as a central and natural solution to economic and social problems. The spread of ICTs fosters inequity in terms of language barriers, geo-ethnic background factors, and Internet access and media literacy. The flow of data does not dissolve existing social structures: if anything, the old structures are reinforced by the new technologies. In this sense, new technologies increase structural inequalities. Technologies and markets on their own are unable to solve the social problems of media culture.

Why is it, then, that the digital divide should be seen as troubling at all? We are inclined to accept the answer provided by Kieron O'Hara and David Stevens. They suggest that ICTs belong to the group of especially important commons, needs and preferences. Without clean water, food and shelter, individuals cannot survive. Without basic (universal) health care and (free) public schooling, it is difficult to pursue other goals in life. And without ICT experience, people are denied the opportunity of full participation in social and political processes. Thus we believe that ICTs should not be a commodity but a commons (O'Hara and Stevens 2006, p. 71).

The information elite use the gap generated by the technologies for their own benefit. Their neo-liberal ideology is based on the capitalist logic of earning, where technology is turned into a necessity, the acquisition of which signifies growth in sales and the birth of new markets. This tendency is exemplified in commercial software, the capitalist tradition of copyright and the high cost of telecommunications infrastructure: factors that make the use of ICTs impossible in poorer countries. This turns economic politics into power politics and a new form of colonialism. Recognising the different viewpoints of the information-rich and the information-poor thus opposes neo-liberalist globalisation and stresses the need for global politics and research as a means of promoting equal opportunities. Though the opening up of the world is a good and important objective, national governments, non-governmental organisations (NGOs) and organisations such as the United Nations constitute necessary instances of control that have the opportunity to advance equal development in the world.

Another perspective, labelled 'visionary utopianism', strives to unravel the ways of thinking described above. It stresses the reconsideration of values and promotes what has been termed 'ICT avant-gardism', the creative and unexpected use of ICTs to support identity politics and many practical aims. Other visionary utopians endorse a complete change of course, seeing information and communication technologies as part of a global conformity project based on capitalist profit-seeking and the war of all against all. This change of course is expected to take place partly with the help of a new world ethics emphasising equality, ecological thinking and tolerance as the most central values. The new paradigm of ICTs would mean the emergence of a humanist ethics in the new technologies and the global openness of scientific information in virtual universities. As a result of these developments, ICTs would no longer function as an instrument of inequality but would serve to unite people's fates in the global village. The viewpoint of visionary utopianism includes the idea of children and young people as our hope for the future, heralding better things to come, as noted by David Buckingham:

Thus, it is argued that computers bring about new forms of learning which transcend the limitations of older methods, particularly 'linear' methods such as print and television. And it is children who are seen to be most responsive to these new approaches: the computer somehow releases their natural creativity and desire to learn, which are apparently blocked and frustrated by old-fashioned methods. (Buckingham 2000, p. 44)

In contrast to this view, children and young people especially are sometimes seen as innocent victims of media powers (see the discussion in Buckingham 2000). This way of thinking evokes all the beasts of the apocalypse and a wealth of other evils to threaten the idealised world of childhood and youth. The breakdown of the nuclear family, teenage pregnancies, venereal diseases, paedophilia, child slavery and child prostitution spreading through the Internet, drug use, youth crime, the degeneration of manners, suicide and religious cults are all seen as problems exacerbated or even inflicted upon us by the world of media. Schools have been transformed into teaching factories incapable of providing young people with the necessary skills and literacies (see also Castells 2001, pp. 259–60). The media, especially commercial television, often feed children disturbing material that they passively absorb and, 'as a result of their developmental stage', are incapable of processing it. From the point of view of commercial media, children and young people are seen as passive recipients of messages, as spellbound viewers and dim-eyed zombies susceptible to a range of addictions from drugs to the media. ICTs steal children from their parents and eliminate the natural life phases of childhood and youth. These are among the primary reasons why we as parents, critical educators, cultural workers and enlightened citizens need to defend public broadcasting and its commercial-free and violence-free contents.

The question of youth and media is a provocative theme; sometimes it is an issue of moral panic in which children and young people are seen as mere victims of ICTs. The term 'moral panic' refers to a situation in which parents and educators fear that children and youth are spoiled by using new information and communication technologies, and in doing so are challenging earlier cultural practices and traditional conceptions. It is useful to remember, however, that in its time, the spread of cinema to a wider audience provoked a panic reaction and inspired a wave of research intended to demonstrate the destructive effects of motion picture viewing. When a television became standard equipment in nearly every home in the West in the 1950s and 1960s, there was further panic. The third moral panic regarding the detrimental nature of ICTs is, of course, occurring as we speak. A sad fact about these panics is that they rarely provoke any debate about real world problems. It may be, however, that moral panics are receding as social reality becomes increasingly pluralistic (see Fornäs 1995).

Whatever the case, the fact is that in the global village young people with their own practices and consumer choices are often in the vanguard of developments in ICT use. A number of thinkers from diverse ideological camps suggest (see Tapscott 1998; Papert 1996; Rushkoff 1996; Katz 1997; Jenkins 1998; Kinder 1999; Giroux 2000b; Buckingham 2000) that children and young people can act as 'oppositional intellectuals' and 'semiotic guerrillas' of the Internet age. Economic visions of the IMF describe providing network connections to the developing corners of the world and advocate a cultural leap directly from agrarian societies to digital and post-industrial societies.

On the other side are a number of critical pedagogues who have always had faith in the wisdom of youth and are now channelling their hopes to the possibilities of using ICTs as a tool for resistance. For the latter, ICTs represent a powerful tool for self-expression, avant-garde digital situationism, semiotic guerilla war, media criticism and influence through media, interaction and research. Some of these scholars (for example, Giroux 1996; McLaren 1995, 1997; Lankshear et al. 1996) adopt a systematically critical attitude toward the capitalist and commercial foundations of media culture by emphasising the following Marxist point, stated here by O'Hara and Stevens:

> For Marx, revolution occurs at many different strata and substrata. The most visible, quick and often bloody manifestation is political revolution

> – the changing of the system of political power and control. But political revolution is carried on the back of a broader social and economic revolution, and, in turn, technological developments that provide new ways of meeting human needs and preferences. These latter manifestations of revolution often occur over a protracted period of time, which may make them less obvious to the casual observer. If a revolution in ICT is truly under way, then it will drive significant changes at the social and political level. ... Even if we reject Marx's extreme deterministic view, the kernel of truth in his insight remains undamaged: technological innovation and economic (and political) change are closely interwoven. The direction of causality may not be as clear cut as Marx opined – it may be bi-directional in that they are mutually reinforcing – but their interdependence is beyond question. (O'Hara and Stevens 2006, p. 129)

In addition, the Marxist critics maintain that not all of media lessons are worth learning. The messages received from media should be critically negotiated nationally, locally and between family members examining the meanings carried by them, whether visible, invisible, public or implicit. It is often argued that young people are not just more familiar with the practices of media culture than their parents and teachers, but also create new media cultures independently of formal pedagogy or curricula. Without underestimating the capabilities of young people, it is reasonable to claim that children and young people are unable to manage their everyday lives on their own. They need to be loved, supported and understood by adults who also provide them with limits and advice. It does not seem likely that global predatory capitalism could fulfil these needs.

In the context of media culture, the basic needs of children and teenagers remain unaffected. In fact, they may even be highlighted. While some are forced to comply with an inhuman pace of work and the resulting socio-psychological anxieties, and others must live in an inhuman limbo under the constant threat of starvation, the meaning and importance of social safety networks and lasting human relationships are bound to increase. The debate on children and young people reflects not just concern for our own lives and the lives of people close to us, but also for the state of the world. The viewpoint on the state of the world and the welfare of people as seen in the above discourses is altered completely when we begin to discuss the problems of media culture as societal concerns affecting the whole world. It is thus our opinion that the discussion on childhood and young people should be broadened to cover the general conditions and structures of life, or, in other words, social justice in a world ruled by global corporations.

Generally speaking, discussion of media culture has largely been US-based and dominated by liberalist viewpoints stressing individual, national or corporate interests. The people actually affected by this network of problems have no voice in the conversation. They live on the other side of the digital divide, without access to the means to power available in the networked world. Critical voices have claimed that in reality there is little intention to demolish the digital divide. It can be narrowed down somewhat, but not enough to lose the economic advantage derived from it. As perceptively noted by Eduardo Galeano (2001, p. 36):

> And don't forget the ferocious protectionism practised by developed countries when it's a matter of what they want most: a monopoly on state-of-the-art technologies, biotechnology, and the knowledge and communications industries. These privileges are defended at all cost so that the North will continue to know and the South will continue to repeat, and thus may it be for centuries upon centuries.

Is a situation where the South would teach and the North would learn completely inconceivable in this respect?

Forms of Digital Divide

All of the international organisations including the EU, the UN, the IMF, the G8 countries and the OECD have expressed their awareness of the fact that the proliferation and use of ICTs form yet another dimension in the division of the world's youth into fortunate and less fortunate ones. As Castells (2001, p. 265) puts it, 'the new techno-economic system seems to induce uneven development, simultaneously increasing wealth and poverty, productivity and social exclusion, with its effects being differ-entially distributed in various areas of the world and in various social groups'. International agencies, both intergovernmental and non-governmental as well as those belonging to the corporate sector, discuss the digital divide and compile charts and agendas for the purpose of bridging it.

In the debate, the concept of the digital divide is used in at least four different ways (Norris 2001, p. 414; Castells 2001, pp. 256–8). First, there is the notion of the global digital divide that is used to refer to the differences in the use of ICTs between people living in different corners of the world. An important dividing line in this respect can be drawn between the rich North and the poor South. From the point of view of economic activity, ICTs are expected to significantly increase the reachability of potential customers in terms of both marketing and direct sales. The Internet is also believed to benefit the development of public services, such as administration, health care and education. The problems that make up the digital divide are being tackled by hundreds of projects carried out by hundreds of governmental and non-governmental organisations around the world.

The second interpretation of the digital divide concerns the unequal opportunities for ICT use within countries. Important factors here are the individual's socio-economic position, level of education and place of residence. The lower the level of income and education and the further away from the capital the locality, the more likely the person is to be excluded from information flows and networks. This type of social stratification is connected with the third version of the digital divide pertaining to democracy and its possibilities after the digital revolution. The theme of the democratic divide is particularly significant with regard to the civic engagement of young people. Opportunities for children and young people to express their ideas and opinions about different issues in society have traditionally been very limited. Often, the means of influencing the world around them have been limited to peer relationships, rebelling against the boredom of school or the perceived constraints of life at home (Buckingham 2000, p. 13). Furthermore, mobile-based interaction through cellular phones between adolescents and their parents tends to diminish productive conflicts between them, thus robbing adolescents of the opportunity to develop their sense of self through such conflicts.

The increasingly mediated and digitalised essence of culture has opened up the world both geographically and socially. Media culture and ICTs do not automatically equal the globalisation of the economy: they also provide new opportunities for engagement and resistance. Yet, for the moment, it is impossible to know what ICT-based democracy and activism will mean in practice, although the global network and e-mail have already in many instances been successfully used for globalised civic activism. In this sense, the Internet is a contested terrain used by both the right and the left, by dominant media corporations from above and by radical media and other activist groups from below. In the likely event that new technologies constitute the dominant forces of tomorrow, 'it is up to critical theorists and activists to illuminate their nature and effects, to demonstrate the threats to democracy and freedom, and to seize opportunities for progressive education and democratization' (Kellner 2000, p. 316).

The discussion on the digital divide has to do with a participation hypothesis according to which ICTs have a dual effect on the participation of people (Norris 2001, p. 195). First, the new opportunities for participation created by ICTs may strengthen the civic engagement of those who are active in this respect to begin with. Second, ICTs may serve to mobilise those who weren't previously interested in any form of political or social engagement. Similarly, people who do not read newspapers or follow the news on television may be drawn in by the opportunity to participate in societal debate through the Internet. However, it is too early to tell whether the participation hypothesis is accurate on either of these counts.

The fourth type of divide concerns the division in technology and knowledge. One characteristic of the development of ICTs is that as one technological gap seems to be narrowing, another opens up. This is due to the rapidity with which the current technology is replaced with new technology. As stated in a maxim termed Moore's law, computing power doubles every 18 months while costs remain constant. Thus, in the opinion of Castells (2001, p. 256), 'it could well happen that while the huddled masses finally have access to the phone-line Internet, the global elites will have already escaped into a higher circle of cyberspace'. Castells' point appears rather cynical as, from the point of view of sustainable global media culture, the real question concerns the type of ICTs that people need and the kind of technology they use in their everyday activities, whether to do with worklife, gaming, personal contacts or schoolwork. Here we encounter a discrepancy between ICT manufacturers operating on the basis of commercial interests and young people driven by the interests central to their lifeworld.

The concept of digital divide also merits some criticism. The use of the concept has certain social consequences: it functions to shape social reality and contains unarticulated value judgements. The danger of shutting out alternative ways of thinking and constructing a uniform vision of culture is implicit. The discussion on the digital divide may in fact serve to perpetuate the myth of an Internet economy based on 'the magic of technology but, more important, upon a belief in capitalism as a fair, rational, and democratic mechanism' (McChesney 1999, p. 121).

In his book on the Internet, Castells (2001, pp. 258–60) unleashes a relatively powerful attack on contemporary educational systems that sustain the digital divide based on the knowledge gap. Castells' critique focuses on the conviction that education and lifelong learning constitute central resources that add to the individual's work qualifications and enhance his or her personal development. In his opinion, most schools in developing countries, but also in the over-developed countries, function more as storage facilities for children and youth. In any global assessment, schools display tremendous variation with regard to teachers' qualifications and other resources. Castells argues that schools have failed to adopt the type of pedagogical thinking required by the Internet era, thinking that originates in the old idea of learning to learn: 'what is really required is the skill to decide what to look for, how to retrieve it, how to process it, and how to use it for the specific task that prompted the search for information'. Resulting from the misery of schools, the task of preparing young people for the new era is left to the homes, a fact that is likely to further add to the disparities in the knowledge, skills and attitudes of children and young people. Along with a number of other ICT enthusiasts, Castells (ibid., p. 269) stresses that postponing the launch of the Internet in developing countries until after having attended to the more pressing difficulties experienced by the population would be a grave mistake. Without an Internet-based economy, writes Castells, there is little chance for any country to survive in the global race.

Sugata Mitra, who leads an Internet project in a slum in India, supports this line of thinking. Although digital appliances are of little use without the ability to read, the notion that only after a global campaign to organise general education for everyone should we contemplate a quantum leap to the digital age does not seem entirely palatable. According to Mitra, synchronicity is important in shaking off colonialist attitudes: 'The information in the Internet should be available as easily as water and electricity. We can't take the attitude that first we need school, then teachers and children who go to school and only then the Internet. Instead, I would say give them the Internet now' (quoted in Tuohinen 2001). It is important to recall, however, that children not only need the resources generated by ICT economy but also require social security and good-quality basic education and healthcare. In this situation, even basic education, learning to learn and reflexivity are not enough. In order to be able to build their lives in the society of the future, young people need to develop a capacity to critically adapt their learning to the prevailing global, societal and local circumstances. Some local projects have indicated that schooling and basic literacy aren't always necessary to increase people's capacity for action. Often, it is possible to depart from very practical problems and to rely on locally accumulated oral tradition combined with a technology suited for the need and use context. As Sanjit Roy, the founder and director of the Barefoot College in rural India, states: 'We have looked at the problems that the poor face from their point of view and not from the point of view of a so-called expert looking from outside … We have come to the conclusion that, using their own knowledge, skills and practical wisdom, it is possible for them to solve their problems themselves' (quoted in Coles 2002, p. 42).

Nabuur, the Global Neighbourhood Network

Nabuur combines the ideas of social networking and volunteer collaboration by offering a 'global neighbour network'. The idea is simple: there are people around the world in need of good neighbours who can help with simple tasks like donating prizes for a competition, translating documents, filming educational videos, finding information, and so on. Nabuur.com provides a way of becoming a neighbour in a village, thus making small-scale development aid and cross-cultural communication easy. In October 2008, the network had over 16,000 neighbours in 182 villages. By relying on volunteer co-operation, Nabuur takes advantage of the fact that peer-to-peer modes of collaboration allow both 'giving without taking' and 'taking without giving', even if both are also idealisations that can never be found in the real world – something that the Nabuur network also clearly demonstrates. Questions of 'ownership' don't enter the discussion: the idea is to help your neighbour even though she might be in another part of the world. Also the limits of digital collaboration are clearly present. If a village in sub-Saharan Africa wants to start beehives for producing honey, someone in the North may provide her knowledge and even details of different designs for hives, but she can't actually help build the thing or even hand over a hammer.
(http://www.nabuur.com)

With regard to the global digital divide, the uptake of ICTs entails a number of practical problems that are particularly relevant in the poorest nations of the world. The primary concern is the lack of money and ICT resources. It is a generally accepted view that the amount of development aid should be at least doubled from the current total of $50 billion (Annan 2002b). According to this view, poor countries need external funding and technological assistance for basic investments before they are capable of functioning independently in the global market (Annan 2002a). Nonetheless, financial aid provided without the teaching of human and property rights is not sufficient: because of corruption, development aid often ends up in hands other than those for whom it was intended. The second problem is also a financial one: the newest ICT applications are far too expensive from the point of view of developing countries. One suggested solution for this has been the utilisation of freeware and the development of devices that are sufficient for the needs of the user without representing the newest and the fastest technology. A commonly acknowledged problem with ICTs is that instead of originating from the actual needs of people, their development is based on the constant pursuit of financial gain.

The third problem is the language used in ICTs. Today, English is the global *lingua franca*. According to estimates, there are some 3,000–4,000 languages in the world, but 80 per cent of all web sites exist in English alone. A number of possible solutions exist for crossing this language barrier. Young people learn languages spontaneously through watching English-language programs produced by multinational media corporations. Schools around the world teach English as the first foreign language. The language barrier can also be overcome through the help of better-skilled individuals, who, like the scribes of the old days, assist others in their community through translating texts from the local language into English, and vice versa (see La Page 2002, p. 44). Young people learn languages more easily than adults and can in many situations function as translators or, more commonly, as interpreters between people speaking different languages.

Thinking optimistically, the problem of the digital divide is seen as being based on 'a technologically deterministic assumption that closing gaps in access to computers will mitigate broader inequalities, an assumption requiring enormous faith in the capacity of a technology to bring about major social change' (Light 2001, p. 723). From a more critical angle it could be conjectured that we are not dealing with technological determinism at all, but have simply encountered a new case of word magic that manages to keep the discussion on global development going while the predators of global economy are allowed to roam free, unhindered by any international regulations.

The World Divided in Two

Because the ICT revolution is such a recent phenomenon, there are no long-term statistics available that would enable conclusions to be drawn on general trends in the development of ICTs. The most relevant worldwide statistics concern the diffusion of the Internet and people's opportunities to connect to the network. As can be expected, the statistics are very general in nature and limited to certain parts of the world, making it impossible to draw worldwide comparisons on young people's use of ICTs. The picture painted by the statistics of the digital divide speaks the same language as all other indicators of the state of the world: it reveals an accelerating tendency towards polarisation. As the Internet is the most central technology in global media culture, observing its use provides some understanding of the proportions of the overall ICT polarisation. Examining the proliferation of Internet use also affords an idea of the overall significance of ICTs for young people on a global scale.

The methods used to measure the number of Internet users vary, and it is worth remembering that the figures always constitute estimates. There is no denying that, in the last five years, the world has witnessed a veritable Internet explosion. In early 1997, the number of Internet users was estimated at fewer than 60 million globally. In 2002, the number of users had grown ten-fold: some 580 million. In less than five years, in early 2007, the world total doubled, to 1.1 billion. Figures from different continents offer a simplified yet revealing picture of the situation: the distribution of Internet users is extremely uneven.

A regional view reveals that the vast majority, that is, about a half (544 million), of all Internet users live in North America and Europe. The number of Internet users in the Asia Pacific region has risen rapidly in recent years from 170 million in 2002 to 390 million in 2007, that is over 35 per cent of all the users. A growing proportion here consists of the Chinese (the proportion has risen from some 57 million users in 2002 to 132 million in 2007), though the number is still relatively small compared to Internet users in Japan (83 million) and South Korea (34 million).

In Latin America, the number of Internet users has grown from 33 million in 2002 to 89 million in 2007. In Africa, there has been an increase from some 6 million to 32 million, which is the highest relative growth rate in this five-year period. The number of Internet users in the Middle East has grown from 5 million to 20 million in the years 2002–07 (see http://www.internetworldstats.com/stats.htm).

The Internet is thus highly illustrative of the differences between the Northern and Southern hemispheres; the statistics reflect an image of a world split in two. Proportionate to the population of the world, the differences are dramatic. The following statement reported by Eduardo Galeano springs to mind: 'Two out of three human beings live in the so-called Third World, but two out of three correspondents of the biggest news agencies work in Europe and the United States' (Galeano 2001, p. 282). Pekka Tarjanne (2002) of the United Nations ICT Task Force has examined the digital divide and the position of young people in a changing world. According to Tarjanne, 'ICT has created a new world of opportunity', but only for the lucky few. The new world has opened up 'to the individuals fortunate enough to be able to access these technologies'. Like many others, Tarjanne believes in the idea of progress accelerated by the Net: 'Without access, history's exponential progress is evolving without global participation, resulting in what we today call the digital divide, one of the glaring inequalities of our modern society.'

Consequently, in the current situation where the Internet reaches less than 10 per cent of the world's population, reducing the digital divide is dependent on 'the participation and support of all players in different sectors of society, including government, the academic world, civil society, the private sector and non-governmental organizations'. Tarjanne expands his view by stating: 'The impact of the information revolution touches all of society, and ... [the revolution] is being led by the young adults of the world, on both sides of the digital divide. Young adults from developing countries are increasingly realizing the wonders of foreign cultures and customs'. Tarjanne sees young people as explorers who, free from economic and cultural binds, look for information in other countries and have grasped the importance of networking in the global labour market of the future: 'The tools of information technology have provided the next generation with faces and customs of alien places ... Universities and small cafés are flooded with young adults attempting to find news not available to them in their city or village. They realize how important this knowledge economy will prove for their future' (ibid.).

This view is close to the idea of cosmopolitanism (Beck 2002), according to which young people in particular feel as one with global processes and phenomena through popular culture. In the words of Beck (ibid., p. 31), 'the sphere of experience, in which we inhabit globally networked life-worlds, is glocal, has become a synthesis of home and non-place, a nowhere place'. However, there are at least two critical issues to bear in mind here. The idea of progress emphasised by Tarjanne can no longer be thought of as a monologic Western formation capable of functioning as a measure of a range of other cultural formations defined as non-Western. Furthermore, we need to be aware of the fact that not all young people have unlimited access to these glocal experiences or the opportunity to speed up on the information superhighway. As to the question of equal opportunities for young people and the quality of their lives, the digital divide between rich and poor countries may well increase.

According to Norris (2001, p. 49), there is nothing new about the absolute differences in media cultural structures between rich and poor countries. The disparities in media cultural possibilities reflect the differences in national income, health care and education. From the viewpoint of diminishing the digital divide, it is disconcerting to realise that even traditional media is not equally distributed around the globe: its use has accumulated to affluent countries. Norris predicts that the Internet is most likely to be adopted in countries where the old media, such as radio and television, are in active use. In other words, Norris sees no easy end to the division between poor Southern countries excluded from information flows and rich Northern countries not only firmly attached to the currents but also controlling them.

The statistical analyses carried out by Norris thus indicate that the problems in the spread of the Internet to developing countries do not result from the medium itself. The differences in the diffusion of the Internet and traditional mass media are the consequences of the profound economical, political, social and educational discrepancies between societies:

> The problem, it appears, is less whether Namibians lack keyboard skills, whether Brazilians find that few websites are available in Portuguese, or whether Bangladesh lacks network connections. Instead, the problems of Internet access are common to the problems of access to other communication and information technologies that have been widely available for decades in the West. (ibid., p. 66)

This being the situation, Norris (ibid., p. 51) recommends the following approach: 'rather than any short-term fix, such as delivering beige desktop PCs to wired schools in Mozambique, Egypt, and Bangladesh, the long-term solution would be general aid, debt relief, and economic investment in developing countries'. She also has this to say about the stages of the Internet revolution (ibid., p. 67):

> In the first decade, the availability of the Internet has therefore reinforced existing economic inequalities, rather than overcoming or transforming them. The reasons are that levels of economic development combined with investments in research and development go a long way toward explaining those countries at the forefront of the Internet revolution and those lagging far, far behind. ... If countries have the income and affluence, then often (but not always) access to the Internet will follow, along with connectivity to telephones, radios, and television.

Norris's argumentation thus departs from that of Castells in a number of important points. Castells sees that efficient utilisation of ICTs can lead to economic success, Norris contends that the uptake of ICTs must be based on a sufficient economic and political foundation. The juxtaposition constitutes a classic chicken-and-egg problem. On the one side, there are the ICT enthusiasts, such as Castells, who argue that access to information sources, particularly the Internet, improves the competitive position of nations and of individuals in the labour market. This blinkered view is, of course, easily exposed when it is considered from a standpoint outside of the Western idea of progress. Moreover, it emphasises the significance of a single type of information: one that is published in the format of bits. Clearly, people's lifeworlds contain many other types of information, such as stories, narratives, music, beliefs, myths, artefacts, tools and local practices of different forms and shapes.

The opposite view is taken by commentators who, like Norris, see that the digital divide cannot be explained through the characteristics of the medium, such as the Internet, or the opportunities provided by it. Instead of linking more schools to the Internet, instructing teachers in issues connected with digital literacy and establishing network connections in poor areas, the focus should first be on the basic tasks such as the realisation of fundamental rights and the elimination of economic, social and educational inequalities.

It does seem, however, that the issue of ICTs provides a seemingly innocuous facade concealing complex political, economic and social problems concerning the state of the world. The idea of bridging the digital divide is an aim supported by many regardless of their political orientation. Discussing the diffusion of ICTs is much more convenient and less conflict-prone than a fundamental debate on major reforms in the global economic and political order. As Light (2001, p. 716) contends:

> It is comforting to imagine that the diffusion and use of a particular technology will remedy complex social problems. ... Certainly, for the myriad of claims makers, the simplicity of the concept and the restricted scope of existing debates are virtues. These simplifications help to generate broad support that more comprehensive constructions of inequality could not.

Here we are again faced with the commonly repeated questions arising from the illusion of progress: the most important of which is, what standard of living can the worlds' resources support? By themselves ICTs are not terribly energy-consuming, but what should we make of the material well being demanded and also created by them? Should ecological values be part of the debate on ICTs? Would it be possible for ICTs to generate a reversal of values that would allow people to see the world as containing differences and different ways of defining concepts such as well being? Perhaps the next direction of ICTs is to be found in sustainable development, where the mass production of new devices in the hope of easy profit would end and young people would no longer be tricked into buying devices in which most of the features are useless. Instead, designers and manufacturers would focus on rolling out simpler and more easily usable technology, as exemplified in products such as the mobile terminal device Simputer (http://www.simputer.org) or the $100 laptop (http://laptop.org).

Information and Communication Technologies as New Forms of Socialisation

Children and young people in the affluent Northern world seem to be living their lives amidst the wonders of media culture. Their media-filled life incorporates the use of ICTs, which is something that they do flexibly in their practices along with other more traditional activities. The mere existence of ICTs makes the lives of today's children and youth differ in important ways from the lives of earlier generations. The products of media culture teach children different attitudes as well as vast amounts of informal skills and knowledge. However, children's everyday learning is often compromised and complicated by the stereotypical attitudes and cultural fantasies of the less-than-ideal adult world (cf. Internet child and teenage porn sites). One might contend that children and youth in ICT-rich countries are currently experiencing the second stage of media culture characterised by two types of phenomena. First, ICTs are used multimodally, which is to say that the different technologies intertwine in many ways in the lives of children and young people. ICTs are mixed together in the Internet (wikis, blogs, in podcasts and video podcasts) and in various mobile devices. Second, the technologies are becoming an increasingly important part of the everyday lives of children and young people, which changes the ways in which young people spend time and interact with people close to them.

In rich countries, children and young people tend to accumulate hobbies (cf. accumulation hypothesis): those who use the Internet seem to be active in other areas of culture (see Suoranta and Lehtimäki 2004). This creates an active group of children and teenagers who are versatile in their use of the new ICTs, but who also participate in sports and culture-related activities. On the other hand, there emerges a group of passive young people, whose everyday life is filled by television viewing, which, incidentally, has been considered as one of the central factors in the diminishing of social capital and solidarity between people (Putnam 2000). Many have argued that in the rich countries of the North, public spaces are disappearing and life in general is undergoing a process of privatisation (ibid.; Giroux 2001), which also entails erosion of social cohesion and trust. As Galeano (2001, p. 274) puts it in his criticism of the present communication world and the unchallenged faith in ICTs:

> This sort of progress just promotes separation. The more relations between people get demonised – they'll give you AIDS, or take away your job, or ransack your house – the more relations with machines get sacralised. The communications industry, that most dynamic sector of the world economy, sells abracadabras that open the doors to a new era in human history. But this so-well-communicated world looks too much like a kingdom of loners and the mute.

An examination of the power relations at work in commercial media opens up another global dimension on the use of ICTs by children and teenagers. The contents of the media culture targeted at children and young people are determined by a small group of global ICT and entertainment companies that dominate the culture industry: Vivendi in Europe and AOL-Time Warner, Walt Disney, Viacom and News Corp. in the US. Relatively unremarked the ICT market is revolving increasingly around children and young people. There are two main reasons for this. One is that children and young people are capable of adopting and, because of their developmental stage, are keen to adopt new things as parts of their lifeworld. The second reason is that children in the affluent Northern societies are becoming an increasingly important consumer group: they have their own money and can also influence their parents' purchasing decisions.

Yet, the vast majority of the children and young people in the world cannot participate in this consumer frenzy: almost half of the world's population has to get by on no more than a few dollars a day, and four out of five under-20-year-olds live in the poor South, and simply cannot conceive of purchasing information and communication technologies for personal use. In this context, the digital divide amounts to nothing more than one more dimension in global inequality.

When discussing young people and ICTs, it is impossible to overlook the fact that young people simultaneously inhabit multiple worlds. On the one hand, they are forced to struggle with a range of vastly different problems concerning livelihood and adjustment. While some toil in conditions best described as slavery and inhabit shanty villages that have sprung up on the outskirts of a metropolis, others contemplate their identities in their bedrooms, chatting away on personal computers. While some strive to escape the authority of parents, others look for someone to offer security and consolation. On the other hand, the youth of today are also faced with the global world. For them, global media culture represents a unifying force, a type of cultural pedagogy that educates them in how to consume, act, 'and what to think, feel, believe, fear, and desire' (Kellner 1995, p. xiii). It is possible, and even very likely, that young people throughout the world are dreaming about the glamorous life of a pop star or a top athlete. In any case, global media culture filled with popular culture is bumping against the real world adolescents live in like a pressure wave. The pressure for homogenisation effected by media culture varies from one culture to another and depends on the young person's media competence and his or her power to resist outside influences.

Culture permeated by ICTs creates a setting where the traditional modes of socialisation are altered and, at least to an extent, replaced with new ones. In the case of ICT use the socialisation process has been turned upside down, as children teach their parents and grandparents. In today's world, mediated popular culture and ICTs constitute a socialising force more powerful than the home or school. It makes sense to perceive the relationship between people and technologies as a two-way one. People invent, use, appropriate and modify technology. Yet, through using technology we learn to live with it, and in this way it makes us the historical beings that we are. This can be seen to constitute dialectical socialisation, where we create technological environments, which, in turn, create us. This is the central lesson of the social history of technology.

In this fundamental sense, it is possible to accept that a person's lifespan and general circumstances are dependent on the time and place of birth. It can be concluded that life is largely determined by demographical, generational and geographical as well as cultural and political factors. This results in a situation where different generations are living as if in different historical eras even in the same countries. Another consequence of this is that the living conditions and opportunities of young people vary greatly. Above, the meaning of ICTs has been observed from a quantitative and rather a general viewpoint. It is important to recall, however, that, above all, the emergence of ICTs is a cultural phenomenon. As Light (2001, p. 711) reminds us: 'Technology is not a neutral tool with universal effects, but rather a medium with consequences that are significantly shaped by the historical, social, and cultural context of its use.' This means that ICTs should always be examined contextually or socio-historically: in this instance, as a part of the changes that have occurred in the lifeworld of young people.

The three-way division of culture into post-figurative, co-figurative and prefigurative by Margaret Mead (1971) provides an interesting opportunity for this kind of examination. The three abstract cultural forms do not form a clear temporal continuum but can co-exist simultaneously in different parts of the world, as, in fact, is the present situation. In a post-figurative culture, socialisation occurs from the older generation to the younger. In a co-figurative culture, people also learn from peers and organise a versatile formal education. In a prefigurative culture, the direction of socialisation changes so that the younger generation may instruct the older generation in how to function in a new cultural situation. The mere speed of cultural change is an important reason for this reversal. In a new cultural situation, old skills, knowledge and attitudes lose their meaning. Naturally, the transformation is never complete: even in a society thoroughly permeated by ICTs, post- and co-figurative cultures continue to live on as traditions nurtured by people.

However, considering the present cultural position of young people, the notion of a prefigurative form of culture acquires new importance, for its central idea corresponds to what has been called global media culture. The assumption that in prefigurative media culture, socialisation would occur exclusively from the immaturity of childhood to the maturity of adulthood, is clearly problematic. The problem is contained in the essence of culture itself. In post- and co-figurative cultural forms, it was possible for culture to be transmitted exclusively from the older generation to the younger. In a media culture, the situation has altered, as cultural transmission can no longer take place just from the old to the young, but also occurs the other way round. Accelerating cultural change encourages two-way socialisation. Popular stories and narratives become a part of the experiences of childhood and youth, while at the same time young people become a part of the narratives of popular culture.

This type of cultural change also explains why the cultural practices and meanings generated by children and young people need to be listened to, read, explored and studied with particular sensitivity. As a part of the lifeworld of children and teenagers, ICTs create public spaces where new associations are formed between knowledge, skill and pleasure (Giroux 2000a, p. 30). In a critique departing from the notion of the two-way socialisation prevalent in the prefigurative culture, school is seen as an institution that both upholds and reforms tradition. School is a sanctuary of closed knowledge, protecting its educational autonomy with every means available. The closed code of school can be compared, for instance, to the open code of the Internet. For the media-savvy teacher, ICTs constitute a never-ending source of information and pedagogical challenges, as they provide the opportunity for establishing virtual classrooms uniting school classes in different parts the world. In the progressive school, ICTs might serve a fundamental pedagogic purpose: to generate discussion across all barriers. The purpose is not to persuade those who think, act and look differently to conform, but to look for opportunities for a common understanding and a better future together.

It is interesting to consider the unprecedented range of opportunities for learning offered by the use of ICTs: young people use ICTs in searching for information using web engines or traditional electronic databases; surfing the Internet as a leisure activity; listening to music in digital format; writing e-mails; engaging in an on-line chat session; attending a virtual school; playing virtual reality games; studying via diverse forms of distance education or participating in projects that call for organisational learning with the help of different information and communication media. The literacy requirements of media culture expand from the ability to read text to capacities to operate and understand the meanings delivered by a variety of equipment (CD and other music players, the computer, the mobile phone, the video), something that often precedes the acquisition of traditional literacy. In addition, it is possible to conceive of on-line chat as a pedagogical site that enables learning in fields such as skilled use of words, interaction unattached to gender and demarcations crucial for identity work. The sending of text messages on the mobile phone produces its own medialore and in its way functions to reform the language, whereas gaming culture enhances sensory and aesthetic perception and produces cognitive skills that have so far been studied very little but have already been shown to provide access to the digital future. Increasingly affordable computers and powerful and versatile software enable young people to remix their own music in cheap self-made studios. Furthermore, a range of subcultures is springing up around globally and ethically compelling issues and appears to be spontaneously generating new forms of communication.

> **ccMixter**
>
> ccMixter is a community site for collaborating on music remixing. Users can upload music tracks, including a cappella vocal tracks; these tracks can be downloaded and mixed together with other tracks, making new songs that can again be uploaded to the site. The content is released under a creative commons licence that makes reuse and remixing possible. The site facilitates sampling, interaction between users and the reuse of remixes. As with the case of free/open source software, ccMixter music can also be marketed commercially, and several ccMixter artists have record contracts.
>
> The costs of the site have been paid by the Creative Commons project; there are no advertisements on the site.
> (http://ccmixter.org/)

According to Willis (2000, pp. 124–5), confidence in one's own skills and the motivation for the creative learning that occurs in media culture arise from creative consumption, fandom and the copying of pleasure-generating cultural products. Learning based on the consumption of culture should be perceived as a normal way to learn, and no distinction should be made between production and consumption in this context. Cultural practices are the practices of learning, and learning – even in school settings – is filled with media cultural meanings. According to Willis, we really are on the verge of a new electronic folk age. The prefigurative media culture has important implications for the position of young people in the labour market. Young people seem to take in knowledge, skills and attitudes from media culture almost by osmosis. Some of these skills are extremely useful in a prefigurative culture: language skills become tradeable assets and computer literacy is hard currency in ICT companies investing in the field. In other words, the new qualifications acquired through informal learning create a more skilled and knowledgeable labour force.

Moreover, the attitudes fostered by media culture have functioned to mould young people into compliant consumers of the future. As concluded by Naomi Klein (2000, p. 275), it seems that brand-name corporations, who have targeted their offers and goods to young people, are abandoning youth 'at the very moment as youth culture is being sought out for more aggressive branding than ever before'. Equipped with skills and attitudes necessary for survival in media culture, young people have become the targets of unparalleled exploitation: 'Youth style and attitude are among the most effective wealth generators in our entertainment economy, but real live youth are being used around the world to pioneer a new kind of disposable workforce' (ibid.).

The ideology of flexibility promoted by the market has placed young people in a difficult position. By attaching their identities to popular cultural messages, they have adopted some of the ideals and ways of thinking promoted by media culture. Yet they are currently finding themselves in a situation where it is impossible to feel secure enough to make any long-term plans, let alone model their lives and futures according to the ideals adopted from the media: 'A hit soap opera is generally the only place in the world where Cinderella marries the prince, evil is punished and good rewarded, the blind recover their sight, and the poorest of the poor receive an inheritance that turns them into the richest of the rich' (Galeano 2001, p. 301). Some proponents of privatisation stressing the viewpoint of capital perceive the situation based on endless flexibility and insecurity as ideal. They should perhaps be reminded that the price of this insecurity is paid in violent behaviour, psychological exhaustion, social maladjustment and general restlessness in society. As Robins and Webster (1999, p. 172) state: 'The race is on to establish increasingly individuated work relationships, with labor ideally linked on a network which allows him/her to be constantly and routinely monitored, while also supplied with the technological know-how and motivational characteristics to allow self-stimulation and autonomous development.'

The construction of a new, individualistic work culture is founded on the promulgation of a new philosophy of education. The principles of this philosophy can be summarised as follows: rather than subjects, young people are taught competencies and skills; teaching occurs by means of problem-solving methods rather than didactic principles; individual learning contracts oblige students to assume responsibility for their own development; there is an increased emphasis on business training and more co-operation between schools and business companies, and a stress on the importance of technology education and computer literacy as well as a commitment to corporative lifelong learning perceived as imperative for success in working life (ibid., pp. 172–3). In this discussion, young people easily become defined as mere instruments of economic activity. Their value is often determined by the extent to which they can benefit the culture of corporations, a concept that refers to 'an ensemble of ideological and institutional forces that functions politically and pedagogically to both govern organizational life through senior managerial control and to produce compliant workers, depoliticized consumers, and passive citizens' (Giroux 2000a, p. 41).

The relationships and causalities between ICTs, young people and the economy are often observed slightly too deterministically. It is claimed that the success of ICT companies has a direct effect on the growth of the economy and thus the well being of young people. In reality the relationship is reversed. Generally speaking, the social infrastructure of society (democratic government, even distribution of income, social security and public services) must be intact to enable the adoption and utilisation of ICTs for the purpose of enhancing sustainable development to the benefit of everyone.

It seems reasonable to claim that the mediated practices of young people, at least in the affluent West, point towards a phenomenon called network sociality. The concept of network sociality can be understood in contrast to the idea of community. The notion of community evokes meanings such as stability, coherence, common history, embeddedness, belonging and a certain social recognition (Wittel 2001, p. 51). It involves strong interaction and longlasting ties as well as rich collective narratives. Conversely, network sociality is not based on a common narrative but on informational acts; as observed by Andreas Wittel (ibid.), network sociality is 'not based on mutual experience or common history, but primarily on an exchange of data'. In network sociality the social bond is created on a project-by-project basis.

The information and communication technologies and media culture in general shape the thinking of children and young people, as they create their understanding of themselves and others in close interaction with ICTs and the messages carried by them. Thus, in a pessimistic interpretation, it is possible to claim that we are moving towards a mode of sociality that is likely significantly to narrow the relationship between a child and his or her caretakers. Furthermore, sociality maintained via ICTs erodes enduring relationships and alienates people from each other. Richard Sennett (1998) has been one of the most prominent social critics of the decline of lasting and trustful relationships. He argues that a flexible project-to-project life without routines and security leads to the erosion of commitment and trust both at work and in family life. These losses then turn into psychological and social pathologies such as forced loneliness and violent behaviour, and other everyday problems ranging from social exclusion to racist stigmatisation.

However, there is also a positive interpretation of the current situation. Margaret Mead (1971) was among the first optimists to suggest that the new prefigurative era carried with it a seed of change for a better future. In her view, the new era necessitated a number of shifts in social relations between people. In the new era the learning process has been turned upside down. For the first time in the history of humanity, children are afforded the opportunity and the responsibility to teach their parents and teachers, to guide their elders on their way to the future.

In a similar vein, Norris (2001, p. 84) mentions generational differences as the most important in the adoption of ICTs. An interesting point in Norris's analysis is that when looking for explanations for Internet use, a person's generation surpasses factors such as income, education and profession. In other words, the cultural and social capital and material resources available to the individual do not mean everything: 'The Napster generation is already experiencing a virtual world as they develop that is different from [the] formative lives of their parents and grandparents' (ibid., p. 85). Thus, the young are not just experiencing the new era, but are also actively shaping the future with their digital

> **WikiEducator, Free e-Learning Content**
>
> The WikiEducator is a community for the collaborative planning of education projects linked with the development of free content for e-learning. The WikiEducator community believes in the social inclusion and participation of all people in networked society, in the freedoms of all educators to teach with the technologies and contents of their choice. It is also assumed that educational content is unique – and by working together people can improve the technologies as well as the reusability of digital learning resources.
> (http://www.wikieducator.org)

practices. Mead (1971) suggests that as adults we, too, must teach ourselves to change our behaviour and give up old ways of thinking in order to keep our minds open to new ideas produced by the younger generation. According to her, only by developing new ways of communicating and new modes of interaction is it possible to free people's imagination from the past. It is her conviction that the development of culture is dependent on a continuous dialogue between younger and older generations.

The dialogue between generations can occur in many ways: the use of ICTs is one possibility if, at the same time, it is remembered that communication over distance can never replace flesh-and-blood interaction. Physical closeness and face-to-face interaction are necessary and important in nurturing relationships not only between the child and the caretaker but also between adults. In the prefigurative age of media culture, it is highly probable that, as Mead suggest, the competencies necessary in media cultures are best achieved through parent–adolescent, teacher–adolescent and parent–teacher dialogue, where young people get to be heard as experts and as teachers, too. For, in the present media culture, it should be imperative for parents and teachers to perceive children's and young people's informal skills in the use of ICTs not as threats, but as opportunities for personal growth and social change and as gateways to mutual respect.

5

EDUTOPIAS AND ACTIVE CITIZENSHIP

It is clear that young people are learning new skills and attitudes in the spheres outside the classroom, and thus the internal and external freedoms of wikipedias, the possibilities for forking and for collaborative and processual content creation, will lead to a complete re-evaluation of the institutions of education. As noted, already Wikipedia content is replacing the need for 'information-delivery' lectures. What is the best way of using time when students and teachers are gathered together in a situation where wiki tools exist? What is the best way of using time when students and teachers are gathered together in a situation where a relatively complete Wikipedia exists? In a few decades, there will be no need to lecture in order to transfer information. Rather, people gathered together can overcome the limitations of cyberspace by discussing, criticising, arguing, synthesising and building an understanding. What is the role of the teacher or any other expert in such a situation? These are the questions we should be asking ourselves while charting a route towards future critical pedagogy. Do we still need higher education institutions with their campuses and related infrastructure, or can we put them to better use, for the people's needs in the Marxist sense of the word?

The situation reminds us of visions launched by many late twentieth-century thinkers (including authors otherwise as different as Jean-François Lyotard and Douglas Rushkoff) who maintained that technologies of various kinds would play an important part in the democratic society to come. It seemed as if new information technologies were fulfilling early prophesies of democratic utopias. John Dewey's pedagogical ideas revolved around the notion of an 'associated life', a blanket term for all sorts of educational ideas and practices, old and new, in which people depend on one another and learn with one another (Bruffee 1995). Ivan Illich (1980), for his part, talked about convivial society, networked communities with their autonomous free street-corner learning clubs and learning webs in which people would enjoy media and create their own contents and messages. Using Gilles Deleuze and Félix Guattari's (1987) concept of rhizome, the basic division in the politico-educational arena can be identified between hierarchal democracy and rhizome-like democracy (Vail 2005), characterised as a 'subterranean root-like stem that builds up a network of interconnections with no central organization' (Morss 2003, p. 134). The division between hierarchical tree-like democracy and rhizomean democracy not only has political implications in the ideas of 'leaderless revolution' and networked dissidence but also has educational implications in how to organise curricula in an era characterised by the end of foundational epistemology. In this situation, teaching cannot easily be seen as an authoritarian activity but more like 'subversive activity' (Postman and Weingartner 1971) in which teachers along with their students compare information from various sources, negotiate their knowledge and experiences together, and interpret the world.

When Jean-François Lyotard (1984, p. 53) claimed that 'the age of the Professor' is ending, he meant that academic professionals and other experts (in their often exclusive ivory towers) are no longer 'more competent than memory bank networks in transmitting established knowledge, no more competent than interdisciplinary teams in imagining new moves or new games'. Think of the team compiling the *Encyclopaedia Britannica* compared to the team compiling the Wikipedia. Lyotard saw only two options for the future of higher education: 'teaching machines', data banks and sorts providing a passive or 'digestive' option, or a more active version, in which creative teamwork would form the kernel of the production of new knowledge. The latter option was in Lyotard's view an elitist version of the future, reserved only for the chosen ones inside academia.

In the Wikiworld the situation is rather different. For Lyotard could not take into account the possibility of using collaborative media, like wikis, in which the former 'memory bank networks' could be actively used and defined almost as 'live' partners in human networks. This, however, is lived reality in the case of today's modes of co-operation between students and teachers, and between citizens and activists of various kinds in their daily studies and the search for the good and just society, as well as in pursuit of new ideas, information, innovations, social justice, peace, knowledge, love and wisdom. Michel Foucault (1988), for his part, once dreamt about diverse methods of critical communication and broadcasting:

> I dream of a new age of curiosity. We have the technical means for it; the desire is there; the things to be known are infinite; the people who can employ themselves at this task exist. Why do we suffer? From too little: from channels that are too narrow, skimpy, quasi-monopolistic, insufficient. There is no point in adopting a protectionist attitude, to prevent 'bad' information from invading and suffocating the 'good.' Rather, we must multiply the paths and the possibilities of comings and goings.

These educational utopias have since been reproduced in a plethora of visions, including our own, that of 'digital social creativity'. However, the utopias are in sharp contrast with present-day university policies and discourses in the Western world. We are repeatedly told that higher education is in crisis due to lack of public funding. As Mary Evans has put it in her *Killing Thinking. The Death of the Universities*, the end of the second millennium 'has not been a happy time, since those years have seen the transformation of teaching in universities into the painting-by-numbers exercise of the hand-out culture and of much research into an atavistic battle for funds' (Evans 2004).

The university system is regarded as our best resource not only for intellectual vitality and creativity but also more straightforwardly for economic competitiveness in global markets. Yet those potential resources are increasingly marginalised by cultures of assessment and regulation (ibid.). The crucial hegemonic struggle concerns the language implicit in the use of the new information and communication technologies. Whose language is it? The language of technocrats, students or teachers? Are there many languages, many vocabularies? Who has the power to define the leading vocabulary? There is a threat that the very same forces that are managerialising and thus ruining the critical potential of the universities will set the standards for language proper. Thus an initial resistance would be urgent; it could start as 'a refusal of a language now inflicted upon university staff' (ibid., p. 74). In this refusal, 'out would go consumers, mission statements, aims and objectives and all the widely loathed, and derided, vocabulary of the contemporary university. In could come students and reading lists' (ibid.). To the 'in-list' we would include the use of social media in their various forms, and enough time for discussion, reflection and debate. A step in this direction is Wikiversity.

Wikiversity

Wikiversity is a project of the Wikimedia Foundation launched in June 2006. According to the project proposal Wikiversity is a network of communities – some local, some global. It is their repository of free, multilingual materials. Wikiversity is an effort to improve the tools which help groups of remote collaborators and their interested communities to create and share an understanding about a subject or an event. The construction and remix of materials is led by people who may be experts or learners. Furthermore the Wikiversity community defines Wikiversity to be 'a sustainable centre for the creation, use and reuse, and dissemination of free learning materials and events'. Its goals are as follows: to collaborate in the creation and hosting of a range of free, multilingual learning materials; for all age groups, in all languages, to host learning communities whose projects share an understanding about these materials, and to develop existing Wikimedia projects. (See also Leinonen et al. 2007.)
(http://en.wikiversity.org)

The institution of education as an invention of the modern era was intended to educate the people as citizens. At the same time as it was supposed to guide them, it also governed and disciplined them. But education – as well as literacy – is more or less a double-edged sword. As Raymond Williams nicely puts it in his book *Television*, if you teach people to read the Bible, you cannot stop them from reading the radical press: 'A controlled intention became an uncontrolled effect' (Williams 2005, p. 135). Whereas modern education emphasised obedience to authority, mostly 'rote memorization, and what Freire called the "banking concept" of education, in which learned teachers deposit knowledge into passive students, inculcating conformity, subordination, and normalization' (Kellner 2004, pp. 10–11), in today's education the emphasis should be elsewhere, for today it is practically impossible to control learning by the means of formal education. Therefore we should now reach for and foster digitalised ways to learn and communicate in co-operation with each other; these skills we can call collaborative literacies.

In terms of literacies, modern education imposed dominant forms of literacy 'associated with formal organizations, such as those of the school, the church, the work-place, the legal system, commerce, medical and welfare bureaucracies' (Hamilton 2005). 'In dominant literacies there are professional experts and teachers through whom access to knowledge is controlled. To the extent that we can group these dominant literacies together, they are given high value, legally and culturally. Dominant literacies are powerful in proportion to the power of the institution that shapes them' (ibid.).

In contrast, what Mary Hamilton terms 'vernacular literacies', and we call 'collaborative literacies', are literacies 'which are not regulated or systematized by the formal rules and procedures of social institutions but have their origin in the purposes of everyday life' (ibid.). Collaborative literacy practices develop, and are learnt informally. They are rooted in action, but are not valued by formal social institutions. Often they develop in critical responses to authoritarian regimes and are part of the local and global protests against the institutions of power. Hamilton (ibid., p. 5) describes these literacies as follows:

Vernacular literacies are as diverse as social practices are. They are hybrid in origin, part of a 'Do-It-Yourself' culture and often it is clear that a particular activity may be classified in more than one way since people may have a mixture of motives for taking part in a given literacy activity. Preparing a residents association newsletter, for instance, can be a social activity, it can be part of leisure or political activity, and it may involve personal sense-making. They are part of a 'Do-It-Yourself' culture that incorporates whatever materials and resources are available and combines them in novel ways. Spoken language, print and other media are integrated; literacy is integrated with other symbolic systems, such as numeracy, and visual semiotics. Different topics and activities can occur together, making it hard to identify the boundaries of a single literacy event or practice. This is in contrast to many school practices, where learning is separated from use, divided up into academically defined subject areas, disciplines and specialisms, and where knowledge is often made explicit within particular interactive routines, is reflected upon, and is open to evaluation through the testing of disembedded skills.

In order to develop collaborative and vernacular literacies as part of political protests as well as participatory democracy and lifelong trans- formative learning, we should increase physical spaces for people and groups to meet and exchange ideas, and as access points for information (libraries, cyber cafés, bookshops, advice centres, Internet buses, community halls) so that citizens can engage in virtual or actual meetings with each other and with experts; strengthen open local government structures and forms of participatory democracy that facilitate social change and citizen action; support local media which help to break the power of the media giants; and provide structured opportunities to learn both content and process skills and link up with others interested in the same issues.

Has Meaning Been Lost from Higher Education?

We want to defend the following argument: It is possible to reinvigorate higher education's critical and revolutionary function by using digital information and communication technologies wisely to create abilities or literacies – what we would like to call 'digital social creativities'.

This debate has levels within levels, and discourses within discourses. Three major positions can be identified: first, those who look at this crisis from the point of the view of educational and financial policy making; second, those who see it from the vantage point of structures and administration; and third, those who define it as part of such mega-trends as capitalist globalisation (Burbules and Torres 2000; Bok 2003; Noble 2003, for example). As William Tabb (2001) has put it:

> When people think about globalization, most focus on sweatshop labor and the loss of manufacturing jobs over-seas. It is easy to understand the race to the bottom that results as factory workers in one place face more intense competition from lower-cost labor on the other side of the world. College teachers would do well, however, to include their own future prospects as they consider the impact of globalization over the coming years. The university will be a very different place in another decade or two, and what it will look like depends to a large degree on what version of globalization wins out.

Broadly speaking, higher education seems to be in crisis, at least in terms of economics, structural matters, demographics, epistemology and pedagogy. These crises take different forms in different academic and other contexts, and they vary between countries, but common characteristics have to do with economics and accountability, and also with the idea of knowledge as a commodity. These are variants of recent capitalist tendencies in global economics, in national public sectors, and in universities as 'diploma mills'. Corporate capitalism has established itself inside academia in the form of a 'neo-liberal model of education'.

Critical scholars have feared that traditional values of Western autonomous academia will be replaced by elements of the neo-liberal model: 'making the provision of education more cost-efficient by commodifying the product; testing performance by standardizing the experience in a way that allows for multiple-choice testing of results; and focusing on marketable skills' (ibid.). As Tabb further notes, at the moment these neo-liberal principles are manifested as 'cutbacks in the public sector, closing "inefficient" programs that don't directly meet business needs for a trained workforce' (ibid.), and in higher education courses and degrees being sold and packaged for delivery over the Internet. As many scholars have suggested, universities have suffered major structural changes in the name of business-like efficiency that has had profound implications for critical inquiry (Huff 2006, p. 30). Furthermore, the priorities and principles of universities 'are being subtly and not so subtly shifted by the exigencies of corporate capitalism' (ibid.). In addition to 'diminished funding for higher education, proliferation of programs and new demands for student-oriented consumer services, there is a crisis of legitimacy that goes to the heart of the academic enterprise' (ibid.).

Part of the talk about crisis is nothing but right-wing gimmickry, another attempt to silence more liberal and critical voices. But an important part of the discussion has to do with a question that we as critical scholars ought to be able to answer: In what sort of a world are we living, and what kind of a world would we want? Or, to put it in pedagogical language: What are our goals in teaching and learning? Part of the crisis critical scholars refer to is the fact that a blind drive for measurement, evaluation and accountability in academic work has pushed these essential questions to the margin. And, who knows?, maybe this has been the very purpose, or at least a hidden agenda, of various US-based conservative think tanks. These, along with conservative forces in academia, push the standardisation of learning and teaching forward, and want to run the university in 'having mode' (Fromm 1963).

The Promise of Digital Social Creativity as Collaborative Learning

New digital ICTs are, at least in the affluent West, creating a phenomenon called 'network sociality'. It can be understood in contrast to the idea of community, which involves strong interaction and longlasting ties as well as rich collective narratives. Conversely, network sociality is not based on a common narrative but on various informational acts. In network sociality, the social bond is created on a project-by-project basis. In pessimistic interpretations, this mode of sociality is seen as diminishing people's opportunities for social and political interaction: sociality maintained via ICTs threatens to erode enduring relationships and alienate people from one another.

As we saw above, in more positive interpretations, it is suggested that the learning process has been turned upside down. Children and young people are afforded the opportunity and the responsibility to teach their parents and teachers, to guide their elders. For example, when looking at explanations for Internet use, a person's generation surpasses factors such as income, education and profession. In other words, cultural and social capital and material resources of the older generation are not decisive.

Thus, the young are not just experiencing the new era but are also actively shaping the future with their digital practices. In the 'prefigurative age' of the information society, it is highly probable that the necessary social and technical skills are best achieved through diverse dialogues and multiple socialisation: adolescents learn from their peers and teach their teachers and parents. In the following, we are suggesting that the world is turning doubly upside down: first, the younger generations have an unusually strong role in creating the future and guiding their elders; and, second, informal education in peer groups, be they virtual or not, is needed to give vital feedback to institutions of formal education.

Media and educational researchers Colin Lankshear and Michele Knobel (2006) have characterised the new digital age in various dimensions as two different mindsets, or attitudes. In Mindset 1, emphasis is on a business-as-usual way of looking at the world, whereas Mindset 2 tries to find new concepts, vocabularies and practices to capture the reality of social digital creativity (see Table 5.1).

The qualitatively new features of this upside-down world of learning are the digital tools used for open collaboration. It is important to note that these tools are an amalgam of social and technological innovation. For instance, something like the free encyclopaedia, the Wikipedia, needs both technological innovation (wiki software, the Internet, a server park, and so on) and new

Table 5.1   Two Mindsets (adapted from Lankshear and Knobel 2006)

Mindset 1	*Mindset 2*
The world is much the same as before, only now it is more technologised, or technologised in more sophisticated ways	The world is very different from before and largely as a result of the emergence and uptake of digital electronic inter-networked technologies
The world is appropriately interpreted, understood and responded to in broadly physical-industrial terms	The world cannot adequately be interpreted, understood and responded to in physical-industrial terms only
Value is a function of scarcity	Value is a function of dispersion
An 'industrial' view of production – Products as material artefacts – A focus on infrastructure and production units	A 'post-industrial' view of production – Products as enabling services – A focus on leverage and non-finite participation
A focus on individual intelligence	A focus on collective intelligence
Expertise and authority are 'located' in individuals and institutions	Expertise and authority are distributed and collective; hybrid experts
Social relations of 'bookspace'; a stable 'textual order'	Social relations of emerging 'digital media space'; texts in change

socio-cultural practices (a certain 'hacker' relation to information, an attitude of anti-vandalism, informal hierarchies and division of labour, and so on) in order to function. This emerging and rapidly expanding amalgam is the Petri dish for open collaboration and so-called social media, be it in the form of the various types of wikis (Wikipedia, Wikibooks, Wikimedia, and so on), open content production and distribution, social bookmarking, folksonomy (user-generated taxonomy and categorisation), free/open-source software, the blogosphere, and so on. Open collaboration with digital tools is potentially global, transgressing national, racial and economic boundaries. This in itself is already a major challenge for systems of formal education. While the rhetoric of equality, interaction and active citizenship typically dominates the official educational agenda, open collaboration with digital tools is most often part of children's and adolescents' informal education, and, more often than not, also something that seems alien, if not threatening, from the institutional point of view. Consequently, a growing credibility gap is created between the worldview and sociality experienced through peer-induced informal learning and the worldview offered through formal institutional education.

ORSi, the Open Research Swarm in Finland

The Open Research Swarm ORSi is an experimental, self-organising academic research community utilising social media tools. Its main purpose is collectively to achieve rapid solutions to given questions and challenges. ORSi's research work is transparent and it works collaboratively. Like Wikipedia, ORSi is open for everyone to participate in. The questions and research topics come from different sources: from the members, from research programs, or from the general debate in the mass media. ORSi builds on the ideas of open science and open access and open educational resources (OERs). Openness is seen as a broad concept, including the research process, financing and participation. 'The aim of ORSi is to achieve high quality research both academically and ethically. One of the key advantages in the swarm-based collaboration is its agility and easiness of finding the best experts for each research question. That should result in efficient use of resources. Also the results can be published more quickly, when the documentation and reports are openly on the Internet. The quality of the papers is ensured by both internal and external peer review procedure, and the results may be publicly discussed by anyone.'
(http://tutkimus.parvi.fi/index.php/Tutkimusparvi-in-english)

From the point of view of open digital social creativity, it would be desirable to see these two realms – formal and informal learning – in tight interaction with each other in terms of teaching and assessment. One way to make this to happen would be to open up more possibilities for collaborative methods of teaching and learning. This is essential for students of today so that they no longer act as passive recipients, 'empty vessels into which we pour our pearls of sociological wisdom, but as active citizens, capable of absorbing a rich lived experience, participants in public debates they carry beyond the classroom' (Burawoy 2006). In changing our pedagogical habits we need to learn collaborative teaching methods, and in the process learn to 'share our toys' (Bruffee 1995). Using John Dewey's terminology, we should substitute individualistic life for 'associated life'. This might gradually change the way we think, and eventually change the world. The question is, of course, are we ready to change, and, further, why bother? Kenneth Bruffee (1981) has summed up more reasons from the academic point of view:

> Interest in collaborative learning is motivated also by recent challenges to our understanding of what knowledge is. This challenge is being felt throughout the academic disciplines. That is, collaborative learning is related to the social constructionist views promulgated by, among others, the philosopher Richard Rorty (*Philosophy and the Mirror of Nature*) and the anthropologist Clifford Geertz. These writers say (as Geertz puts it in his recent book, *Local Knowledge*) that 'the way we think now' differs in essential ways from the way we thought in the past. Social constructionists tend to assume that knowledge is a social construct and that, as the historian of science Thomas Kuhn has put it, all knowledge, including scientific knowledge, 'is intrinsically the common property of a group or else nothing at all'.

Consider, for instance, the epistemology of the Wikipedia. Though the comparison by Giles (2005) suggests that Wikipedia articles in English in general are comparable to those of the *Encyclopaedia Britannica*, the really revolutionary part of Wikipedia is not connected to peer-group-generated reliability. Rather, first and foremost the fact that articles can be written on almost any topic provides a wide folk-o-pedia with a scope far outstripping that of traditional encyclopaedias. And, in addition, a Wikipedia article always comes with its history and the connected discussions. This 'genealogical' stratum gives it an epistemologically different status from a *Britannica* article. And, as Bruffee (1981) maintains, collaborative learning 'is related to these conceptual changes by virtue of the fact that it assumes learning occurs among persons rather than between a person and things'.

In reflecting on these questions, we should focus on the structures and processes of teaching and learning in the university classroom and ask, are students' superficial attitudes deriving from the teaching methods, and how they are treated in the classroom? Are they kept as objects of teaching, or as co-thinkers and agents who are able to create their own world with their teachers and peers? In answering these questions honestly we have had to admit that our teaching has often been based on what Paulo Freire has referred to as the 'banking method' (Freire 2005). In the banking method, students become alienated and lose interest in learning, for, as Freire put it in his *Pedagogy of the Oppressed* (ibid., ch. 2), it is the omnipotent teacher who knows and students who digest by listening.

> In the banking concept of education, knowledge is a gift bestowed by those who consider themselves knowledge-able upon those whom they consider to know nothing. Projecting an absolute ignorance onto others, a characteristic of the ideology of oppression, negates education and knowledge as processes of inquiry. The teacher presents himself to his students as their necessary opposite; by considering their ignorance absolute, he justifies his own existence. The students, alienated like the slave in the Hegelian dialectic, accept their ignorance as justifying the teacher's existence – but, unlike the slave, they never discover that they educate the teacher.

And, as Freire continues: 'The *raison d'être* of libertarian education, on the other hand, lies in its drive towards reconciliation. Education must begin with the solution of the teacher–student contradiction, by reconciling the poles of the contradiction so that both are simultaneously teachers and students' (ibid.). Alternatives for the banking method are diverse student–student and student–teacher collaborations and encounters.

In collaborative learning, students learn by working with each other on focused, open-ended tasks, discussing issues face to face in small groups. Collaborative learning taps higher education's most powerful yet repeatedly underdeveloped resource: peer-group influence. According to Bruffee (1981, p. 745), the 'primary aim of collaborative learning is to help students test the quality and value of what they know by trying to make sense of it to other people like themselves – their peers'.

In addition, collaborative learning is a viable way to get to know each other in a face-to-face setting; to study some of the basic theories, methods, concepts and contents of a given field; to learn how to do things together ('share our toys'); to develop trust in an open atmosphere; to build 'transgressive', multidisciplinary competencies (Nowotny 2000) needed in various professional practices; to learn how to learn professional interdependence when the stakes are low; and to create a democratic idea of knowledge and research work. By using collaboration, students are introduced to methods of learning, problem-solving and task efficiency that they can later employ in the workplace. Here we are inclined to think like Lyotard (1984, p. 52):

> If education must not only provide for the reproduction of skills, but also for their progress, then it follows that the transmission of knowledge should not be limited to the transmission of information, but should include training in all of the procedures that can increase one's ability to connect the fields jealously guarded from one another by the traditional organization of knowledge.

Let us again think of the Wikipedia as an example of this sort of mixing professions and often tightly gated areas of professional knowledge. In writing Wikipedia text one can contribute and collaborate anonymously without the anticipation of academic or other glory.

In this sense, digital social creativity as collaborative learning is in opposition to capitalist higher education that trains students to individual obedience and reproduction of an organised stock of established knowledge in order to succeed. It is also a counter-argument to the system's continuous emphasis on individualism, relentless competition and accountability creating an ethos of hatred, envy and suspicion. The collective history of a Wikipedia article and the social interaction on which it is based show quite clearly how individualism and malevolent suspicion can be overcome with openness and collective responsibility. This does not mean, however, that criticism is to be precluded: the easy modification of a Wikipedia article promotes a critical and necessary distance for the 'extended' creation of new information and the reproduction of old.

The problem is, of course, that teaching is not usually seen as an important or rewarding part of academic life, but rather a fairly unfulfilling and laborious task, far less important than research and writing. This is unfortunate, for 'faculty members may play the single-most important role in student learning' (Umbach and Wawrzynski 2005, p. 176). Along with personal supervision and mentoring, teaching is the only official way to interact with the younger generation within the university. For that reason alone, we should take the words of Henry Giroux to heart:

> I believe that intellectuals who inhabit our nation's universities should represent the conscience of a society not only because they shape the conditions under which future generations learn about themselves and their relations to others and the outside world, but also because they engage in pedagogical practices that are by their very nature moral and political, rather than simply technical. And at its best, such pedagogy bears witness to the ethical and political dilemmas that animate the broader social landscape. Such pedagogical approaches are important because they provide spaces that are both comforting and unsettling, spaces that both disturb and enlighten. Pedagogy in this instance not only works to shift how students think about the issues affecting their lives and the world at large, but also potentially energizes them to seize such moments as possibilities for acting on the world, engaging it as a matter of politics, power, and social justice. (Giroux 2003b, pp. 194–5)

The Uneasy Relationship between Formal Education and Collaborative Learning

In our view, there are two major reasons for the uneasy relationship between institutions of formal education and the digital environments of open collaboration. First, open collaboration creates a seismic epistemological and ontological shift in the production and legitimation of knowledge. The claim to truth, knowledge and enlightenment that content produced in open collaboration makes is not created through authority, certainty and legitimacy, but through dialogue, perspectivity and pragmatic value in 'imaginative' groups and minds, whether in the universities or elsewhere. For example, the trustworthiness of an entry in the Wikipedia is best evaluated by analysing its history, the amount of criticism and alternative viewpoints to which it has been subjected, and the benefits for the reader.

Wikipedia is a paradigmatic example of the epistemological challenge, because it explicitly deals with knowledge and information, but the same effect is felt in various degrees throughout the field of content distributed and produced through open collaboration. The worldview and 'hidden' messages contained in collaboratively created audio or video content raise the same epistemological questions. A bricolage created by 'rippin and mixin' existing content often self-consciously challenges the presuppositions of classical epistemologies, such as finality, authorship and assent. Teamwork and craftsmanship gain new importance as works of open collaboration resemble the works of Renaissance painters: an entire studio of apprentice scholars of various levels of talent and areas of expertise is involved in the production, more or less closely overseen by a 'master'. Despite their rhetorical commitment to collaborative and interactive learning, institutions of formal education are having a hard time dealing with this epistemological shift.

Second, and not unrelated to the first point, open collaboration and social media emphasise the non-informational uses of ICTs. Think about a teenager creating fan fiction: most likely, he or she will be multitasking with instant messaging, Internet relay chat, blogs related to the theme and other tasks (such as SMS messaging with friends, listening to music, doing homework) all the time. Most of these activities are more readily categorised as social and communicative – having to do with identity, pleasure, entertainment – than as informative or educational. However, the experienced and convivially constructed world in which our fictive author of fan fiction operates, is most intimately also the world in which he or she needs the skills of literacy, criticism and autonomous creation.

Together, these two features, the dialogical nature of knowledge and the emphasis on social interaction, create a tremendous educational opportunity. The platforms of open collaboration are fulfilling several goals of the convivial information society, like those of community and co-operation as key elements of democracy, freedom, openness and transparency, and active participation. However, we need a framework for bridging the gap between informal collaborative learning and formal education, so that they do not, in the worst case, work against each other.

By envisioning a world in which the Wikipedia and various forks of it – for example, wikipedias with different partisan points of view – have existed for decades, we can gain an insight into the shape and function into which formal education should be moulding itself. All experts can be challenged in the blink of an eye by access to the wikipedias. Expertise will be transformed into the skills of grasping wholes and seeing connections, and, most importantly, being able to participate in meaningful and rewarding collaborative work. This transformation, the beginnings of which we are already experiencing when constructing curricula and choosing lecture material, is not well served by restricting access to information and collaboration, be it in the name of safety, control or the protection of intellectual property.

The problem of the credibility gap translates into a concrete question: how to secure the freedom of knowledge creation and learning in the institutions of formal education? But the answer is simple: practice what you preach. Many teachers and educators use open content, such as the Wikipedia, regularly, and participate in open collaboration through the Internet. The next step is to get involved in the collaborative projects and forms of social media in which students are already immersed. This could mean getting involved in the world of digital games, manga, fan fiction or something similar, or it could mean producing a neighbourhood wikipedia or a local podcast.

The attitude for avoiding closed teaching machines is well summarised by the Net pioneer John Perry Barlow (quoted in Beckedahl 2006):

If you wanna share something – share it. If you wanna use something – use it. Try to do so ethically in the sense of don't take things without attribution, attribute. Make sure that the people who did create actually have the opportunity to get some enhanced reputation and, thereby, you know, greater economic return. But … pay no attention to these people when it comes to being creative. Go ahead and do the stuff that Larry showed in the beginning of his talks and do a lot of it. And every time they put a lock on – break it. And every time they pass a new law – break that …

The key is to focus on the content that is actual and relevant, so that the institutional involvement does not occur in an academic vacuum, thus promoting alienation. Institutional involvement can overcome the credibility gap and become a partner in the dialogical epistemology, if and when it has a grounded point of view and a real stake in building a convivial information society for all. Institutions of formal education should be the hubs of open collaboration, instead of turning into gated communities of further segmentation and deepening digital divides. The system logic of formal education needs to be nourished by the logic of collaboration and sharing evident in informal peer-to-peer interaction of the digital world. Hence we cannot but agree with Noam Chomsky's view on the role of the students in learning, a view which echoes Dewey, another master thinker of the twentieth century. Chomsky (2000, p. 21) is worth quoting at length:

One should seek out an audience that matters. In teaching, it is the students. They should not be seen merely as an audience but as a part of a community of common concern in which one hopes to participate constructively. We should be speaking not *to* but *with*. That is second nature to any good teacher, and it should be to any writer and intellectual as well. A good teacher knows that the best way to help students learn is to allow them to find the truth by themselves. Students don't learn by a mere transfer of knowledge, consumed through rote memorization and later regurgitated. True learning comes about through the discovery of truth, not through the imposition of an official truth. That never leads to the development of independent and critical thought. It is the obligation of any teacher to help students discover the truth and not to suppress information and insights that may be embarrassing to the wealthy and powerful people who create, design, and make policies about schools.

But what, then, is the proper pedagogy of helping students to search for truth, and learn freely in the Wikiworlds? At least three tenets must be met when dealing with truly liberatory and transformative pedagogy in higher education. First, it is necessary to build educational activities from below, or 'from the ground upward in a democratic way, with students and teachers as codesigners of the process' (Brookfield 1995, p. 136). This provides them with a 'sense of connectedness' and as a democratic experience in learning instils democratic sentiment. Second, this democratisation of the educational situation is indivisible, for partial democracy is like partial pregnancy – it does not exist. Third, a certain leap of faith is needed in teaching democratically. As Brookfield puts it:

> Once you commit to working democratically, you have to take the leap of faith that says that people will make informed choices. And you must trust that if they don't make the choices that you think in the short term are the best ones for them (like attending every class), in the long run, the experience of being in control will make them more responsible the next time they are able to exercise power. (ibid., p. 137)

Viagra and Active Citizenship

If meaningfulness in life has more or less disappeared, a replacement is found in material, consumerist dreams. And there is no lack of those who offer them. A multitude of industries rake in profits from the manufacture of dreams. The dream society tells of minds yearning to be elsewhere. Meaninglessness must be overcome with the dream of a better, meaningful life. The Hollywood dream factory has always known how to capitalise on this human desire for what is missing in everyday life: a rich, exciting and meaningful existence. But as Richard Dyer, a scholar of popular culture, has observed, Hollywood provides a feeling of what utopia might be like, but it does not realise that utopia. The dream will remain unfulfilled, but you can always buy a new one.

Contemporary culture is often described as visual culture, implying the visibility of cultural signs and messages and the emergence of visual forms of narrative in all areas of communication. Marketing and other messages attracting our attention and guiding us toward consumption have inundated our everyday lives with garish colours and temptations steering our behaviour. Our visual environment is filled with messages in which a strange voice is speaking. Is this the kind of environment we fancy? What if we would like to say something ourselves, to talk about our own experiences in our own voice, and with our own visual messages?

The visual environment in which we live should be everyone's shared environment, a comfortable home. It is, however, often the case that the townscape, for example, is influenced most by other actors, ones for whom the city is primarily a domain for business, and not the living environment of human beings. The city, however, marks the individual and is located in him or her, as part of personal identity, the live world and meaningfulness. Graffiti artists have often tried to change the townscape with alternative messages, albeit not always very successfully. They are regarded as visual troublemakers and terrorists, while a beer ad on a boarding is part of a normal townscape. We happily pay to wear clothing covered with corporate logos and serve as walking advertisements. But what if the T-shirt is a means of personal expression, for stating one's own ideas?

Identity has become a central quest in the dream society. We no longer necessarily know who we are, for we seek meaning in our lives by looking for a new script, and perhaps changing roles and sequels. The pedagogue Thomas Ziehe has noted that in contemporary society it is easy to hope that one is someone else and to expect and imagine more of oneself. One can always want more, and imagine how things could be otherwise. Unlike traditional rural societies, in which the path of one's ancestor had to be followed, life is not preordained. But the above-mentioned 'more' also generates conflict: 'How one could be while not being: what one expected but did not receive, what one wants yet does not want; what one does and therefore cannot do otherwise.'

We can always make comparisons, dream, want more or desire something else. Identities are at stake, changing and moving.

Already in the late 1920s, Martin Heidegger wrote perceptively in *Being and Time* (translation from 1962) about the fundamental form of human existence that he described as the life of *das Man* or 'the they'. It is a life not quite one's own, but instead one of drifting with a crowd – a crowd that is now increasingly being steered by the media and entertainment industry: life depends on the thickness of the wallet. Heidegger writes of actors living just like anyone else, seeing the same art exhibitions as anyone else and even standing out from the crowd just like anyone else. *Das Man* is not quite himself, not finding his own direction in life nor choosing it. Instead, he constructs his identity through forms of existence externally defined, from other people and the models of the media industry. Heidegger's message, however, can only be grasped through personal experience – when one has sunk so deep into the mundane regularities of everyday life that one wakes to the uncomfortable feeling of not being quite present in one's own life, not living one's own unique and ultimately brief life, but seeing instead how one is being pulled by the current and wondering for whose benefit one is actually acting and what sense there is to any of this. For Heidegger, this experience and this awakening are the voice of conscience, a voice not accusing or blaming, but instead seeking a meaning for life, wishing to find something of permanence and value.

Who is the 'active citizen' or 'entrepreneur' that is the ideal in liberal democracies? The person who takes part in politics, civil society and the economy both locally and globally, using all the mechanisms and channels provided by representative democracy, new media and empowerment initiatives? Is it not *das Man*, the tasteless unit of production and policing, who shuns both passion and ideology and all other politically incorrect behaviours in order not to be labelled a Nazi of this or that kind? And is not the *das Man* of information society modelled on necrophilia? Making love to a dead body does not initiate two-way passions or responsibilities (Žižek 2004c). The supporting male-intellectual-hedonistic fantasy of the information society is a cocktail of solitude, silence, drinking, content production, interaction and love-making with a partner that you do not need to face after the act – however kinky (see Beigbeder 2004, p. 76). When the other does not say 'no' and you do not yourself get committed, the fantasy is never challenged – nor made real. While the modern subject saw itself as responsible for its life, the postmodern subject is always a victim of circumstance. Hence the rule: minimise ulteriority, ironise interiority.

The tolerance of liberal democracies and consumerist capitalism cushions the subject from the brute force of the outside world. A description of the everyday of an active citizen might run like this: 'I worked, downloaded porn, masturbated to the usual heteroflicks, even though I didn't find S/M strange in an age where the humiliation and control of people has been made into a cardinal virtue and an official almost constitutional doctrine, I studied, did not throw bombs yet, not even creamcakes' (Seppälä 2004, p. 23). And the work in content production turns into endless 'seminars, centres of excellence, incubators, research, fact-finding, design and development projects, planning and coordination meetings, working groups, steering committees, best practice hunting trips, third sector collaborations, e-learning environment enhancements, pilot projects, investment plans, quality control assessments' (ibid., p. 11). Liberal democracy is its own enemy. It sadistically suffocates resistance while at the same time masochistically proliferating it by ironising, demonising, fencing, thanking, rewarding. *The Truman Show* is a telling allegory of the sadomasochistic pursuit of happiness and of the leaks at the edges. *The Truman Show* effect is everywhere: the nausea felt at supermarkets and malls, being bounced from one help-desk to the next, the locks on the door of retirement homes, two planes embedded in a skyscraper …

The market is ripe for enjoyment without friction, cream without fat, coffee without caffeine, beer without alcohol and sex without a partner (other than the virtual reality dataglove, that interprets motion on-screen). Wars are also without dead (on our side), and politics is without ideologies. As Žižek (2004c) points out, the injunction is to enjoy even more and without guilt:

if by eating too much chocolate you become constipated, there is a laxative chocolate for you! Nothing is too little or too much; we have everything to choose from, and on top of everything sits 'morality, the police, and a condom' (Varto 1995, p. 60). While education used to aim for a golden middle and moderation, now we should consume (eat, drink, fuck, surf) as much as we can!

Does the term 'information society' not itself rely on the virtual nature of 'information'? The information society tolerates everything that stimulates discussion and inclusion. There is no outside, only the growing logistics of information-material-desire. The reflexive modern, the risk society, the information society, are all mystifications of the 'freedom of choice'. What you choose governs who you are, what your world will be like, what is offered to consumers, how much CO_2 is produced, and so on. The other side of consumption is hidden: what you want and the diversity offered are both determined by advertisement. The news in your daily paper or on your RSS feed-reader is not there because it is important; it is important because it is in the news. The freedom of choice and our independence from others ('There is no such thing as society', according to the former British Prime Minister, Margaret Thatcher) is created in the world of ad fantasies, where you buy in order to be free and are free in order to buy. The car, the lipstick, the toothbrush, the hedge fund, all promise liberty, real freedom. As Finnish novelist Juha Seppälä defines it: 'a social democrat is someone who wants freedom in order to get money' (Seppälä 2004, p. 23). The flow of information is closed: we need money in order to buy freedom to make money in order to ... When Marx claimed that the workers in capitalism are not the subjects of their productive activity, Karantani continued: 'If workers can be subjects at all, then as consumers' (quoted in Žižek 2004b, p. 124). But you cannot eat your way to the end of this sausage: we produce what we consume, and the material cycle is mirrored in the circular fantasy of money–freedom–money. This is why we have to ask: Freedom for whom? Freedom to what? And, more particularly, information society for whom, and for what?

The image of the information society is directly linked with new digital media. There the node of 'interactivity' ties together the fantasies of democratic potential, freedom, active citizenship, lifelong learning, new economy, and so on. But interactivity has its shadow, too. First, interactivity, like active citizenship, easily turns into an obligation ('If you can, you must') to interact. Interactivity is the Viagra of the information society – because participation is technologically possible, it must work! And as Viagra recreates sexual guilt ('You can, so you must') (Žižek 1999b), interaction recreates socio-political guilt. This guilt masks a genuine need for interpassivity. In Robert Pfaller's (2000) definition, interpassivity denotes phenomena where an emotionally or cognitively charged task is outsourced to somebody or something else. For example, a prayer mill can keep on praying for me, liberating my subjectivity from the task. Likewise, the true motivation for readymade laughter in TV comedies is interpassivity: I don't have to engage in recognising, sympathising with and interpreting the drama.

However, the need for interpassivity may change into its negative when illusory interactivity produces passivity. Interactive media has its own logic that curtails the functioning of the user, even while at the same time creating an illusion of participation. Žižek's (1999a) favourite example is an elevator, where you can push a button to speed up the closing of the doors – without any results. No matter what you do, the doors close at the same pace. Is this not the experience of representative democracy expressed by a majority of voters, including the non-voters? The interactivity of the information society is of the same kind: you can keep pushing all the buttons and, for example, keep writing about anything; you can say, confess, do anything, as long as what happens is what was going to happen anyway. Everything can be criticised, even 'resisted', as long as the political consensus is not disturbed. All of this happens under a *Denkverbot*, a ban on thinking, where everything is allowed – except taking ideological stands seriously. The hegemonic co-ordinates embrace and include also the myriad social movements, NGOs and aid organisations – from Médecins Sans Frontières to Greenpeace and Red Crescent.

These organisations are not only tolerated, but encouraged by the media. Here interpassivity is political: you keep on doing something in order not to rock the boat. The fervent activity of the multitasking agent of an information society is, to use a metaphor from Arthur Miller, standing still like a hummingbird. The real effects of our activity are outsourced and subjectivity immobilised by the split between what is immediately here (consumption, interaction, techno-utopias) and what has been moved beyond immediate perception (sweatshops, careless pollution, poverty).

While Žižek (2004d) is worried over the new form of racism born in the West – a racism based not on racial or cultural distinctions but on a brazen economical division between the haves and the have-nots – Jean Baudrillard emphasises the spectral-virtual dimension. In his view, the question concerns the balance of the psychology of terror. He sees that global capitalist exploitation is only a medium and an alibi for another, much harsher moral deprivation. Baudrillard concludes that, almost contrary to Marxist analysis, material exploitation only exists as a pretext for spiritual exploitation (Baudrillard 1995, pp. 83–4).

On the one hand, the split is reproduced by the technological utopias of information society and, on the other hand, by televised humanitarian spectacles. The interactivity promised by the utopias and the spectacles mean the endless shuffling of menus on the Net or on your mobile. The matrix is given, now wade through it. When the existence of the matrix is discovered by the subject, interactivity turns into interpassivity. The production of inter-passivity has its micro-level implementation in various media devices and its macro-level structure in the information society. The assumption of the logic of networks and a nomadic identity does not entail 'activity' or 'creativity', but the genuinely passive and reactive choice from a menu.

The closed circle includes research on the information society. For example, research on 'children and ICT' is a morally and socially loaded landmark pointing to a 'life in the information society'. It may happen, for example, that, just as we notice that children immerse themselves in the new media like 'fish in water', the political economy of the information society has already been forgotten. Is there not a similarity to the research topic 'children and war'? When we notice in the study that, despite the war, the kids keep on playing and singing in the ruins of their homes, relativisation and internalisation may begin. Cannot research on the information society likewise produce an interpretation where life in the information society gets more tolerable after every chart and survey?

The still-beating heart of an interactive renaissance through the development of an information society is dependent on actual freedom in the sense of 'reconfiguring the co-ordinates of the possible'. This utopia must be contrasted to interactivity in a hegemonic matrix where interactivity equals interpassivity. Should we not pay attention to the non-voters' message? What if their claim that, in the act of voting, the how (participating in the formal act of interactivity) overshadows the what (who you vote for)? What if even leaving a blank vote means agreeing with the formal conditions of 'interactivity'? Finnish critical sociologist Antti Eskola gave the following answer in the late 1960s:

In the totalitarian society there is hope for it is quite likely that the repressive system eventually collapses, as there is no mechanism for adjusting the political pressures which try to change the system. Thus the pressures accumulate. So-called democratic society is much more dangerous also in this respect. Contradictions, discontent, the experience of inequality and other pressures trying to change the system are cleverly adjusted, dissolved, made ineffective and finally directed to harmless targets. Apparent competition for political power assures the *status quo*. (Eskola 1968, p. 130)

6

STAGES OF FREEDOM:
FROM SOCIAL TO SOCIALIST MEDIA

Behind the veil of a multitude of resistances and critiques, we should see the shape of certain Aristotelean 'movers unmoved' (*primum movens*). Capitalism is one of them; the particularities of the fight by developing countries against prohibitive tolls and tariffs, of the fight by Indian rice farmers against RiceTec and its patents, of the fight against the privatisation of water, of the fight against liberating markets by armed force, constitute, in fact, a generality: the generality of a capitalist mode of production. Current ethnic conflicts point to the same conclusion: the decline and destruction of local cultures is a continuation of the colonisation that swallowed Finland in the thirteenth century and many other 'peripheries' much later. These are not isolated acts of aggression, but are a direct consequence of a sustained Western impulse for trade and conquest.

The other unmoved mover is the West itself. As noted by Chomsky (2001, p. 20), India never attacked England; Congo, Belgium; Ethiopia, Italy; or Algeria, France. This is also why he insists in his book *9-11* that the remarkable thing about 9/11 was that it was a hit by the colonised on the colonist's ground. For the same reason he suggests that we should identify the attacks in spatial terms (New York, Washington, London, and so on), not in temporal ones (9/11, 7/7, and so on). The crucial thing is *where* the attacks happened, not when. Research on the information society should remember this: there are structural similarities in the various information society developments, generalities among particularities. Is the technological control of the globe not one with a specific model of society, namely Western capitalism? Or do we really have modes of technological modernity that are different from the hegemonic Anglo-Saxon one? And does the information society not promise unprecedented technological control? We have to ask, how open or malleable is the capitalist Western information society?

Let us take an example. If digital technology and information are ever more important resources and end results of production, the distribution of technology and information becomes an essential indicator of global equality (either you take part in the networks, or not!). Again, no one is openly promoting a view that digital technologies should profit only the First World, but still the digital divide between North and South keeps growing, despite all the initiatives, leap-frogging, projects and programmes (Suoranta 2003). What structures in the world have, in fact, become more malleable, programmable? And what are the structures that are even more rigid and predetermined?

Jean Baudrillard sees a logical conclusion in the trend of Westernisation. The premise: The West sees the rest of the world as a resource, as the natural producer of commodities. The last in the long chain of commodities is catastrophe, accompanied by a catastrophe aid industry. At least here, says Baudrillard, Marxist analysis holds perfectly true. Misery is reproduced as a symbolic resource, a necessary fuel for the Western moral and sentimental balance. We are the consumers of this spectacle, and the West feeds on catastrophe mediated by cynical news broadcasting and our moralistic humanitarian help. Baudrillard insists that we are just as dependent on this drug, produced by the developing countries, as other drugs (Baudrillard 1995, pp. 84–5). The irony is that global capitalism is strong, dynamic and perverse enough both to produce the drugs it needs and to outsource the misery to the others.

A snippet from the op-ed section of our local newspaper, written by the pseudonymous 'Pessi' (2004):

> I'm bored. Totally helplessly fed up. Bored of the starvation, of Iraq, suicides, racism and Matti Nykänen [a once famous Finnish ski-jumper turned alcoholic, frequently in the tabloids]. ... I'm fed up with perfection, eating

> disorders, pop-stardom, single mothers, family violence and chewing gum on the chairs in the cinema. I'm bored with being bored and bored with the feeling that everything that happens, happens at the wrong time and to the wrong person.

Is this not a succinct description of the Baudrillardian produced catastrophe, the continual media massage? Is this not the *Zeitgeist* of liberal democracies? Is it not also an extreme experience, where the measure and balance of all things is dissolved? Is the existence described by Pessi not a perfect allegory for a run-of-the-mill news programme and the information society as a whole?

But Baudrillard goes on to claim that global capitalism has a rotten core containing the seed of its own destruction. The market for catastrophe will face a crisis with the inevitability that all markets crash. The outsourced catastrophes will finish, which means that the catastrophe has to be produced domestically, since the desire for spectacle and greed for the symbolic is even more natural than gluttony. Baudrillard predicts that the big symbolic crash will be the product of our Western generosity, but it will arrive only after we cannot feed any longer on the hallucinatory suffering abroad (ibid., p. 85).

The crash seems to be far off, however. The disaster show produced by the hybrid White House–Hollywood and shot in the Third and Fourth Worlds goes on. The underdeveloped countries lead the developed countries in the drama of misery by 6–0. The victims of New York, Madrid and the coalition of the willing are in the thousands, while the civilian victims in Iraq are in the hundreds of thousands. But Baudrillard insists that the controlled and produced disaster of the West is more spectacular. As Baudrillard says, we are haunted by overload, boredom, the abundance of possibilities, neurosis and psychodrama – a drama born out of too many means compared to reasonable ends – and this always beats the drama of poverty, deprivation and misery. This is, according to Baudrillard, the primary reason for the possibility of immediate catastrophe in the societies without empty spaces (ibid., p. 87).

The current state in the race towards the bottom is the leakage or explosion of outsourced disaster back to the West. The spectacle is smuggled back to the trains and planes taking the middle class from work to home. The messengers of mediated disaster – Euro MPs and local politicians – speak of terrorism as some sort of metaphysical random evil that is able to strike anywhere at any time in the name of 'curtailing the possibility of the Western democracies to take initiatives in solving the problems of the world' (Kauppi and Stubb 2004). What this view fails to see is that terrorism is a feedback loop in capitalism itself; the calculated re-import of a Western logic and export. Al Qaida, if anything, is the prime example of a network of networks, embedded in the cashflows produced by oil and drug addiction. As Jacques Derrida points out, Osama bin Laden stands on the same power-capitalistic grounds as the World Trade Center towers (Borradori 2003, pp. 95–115).

Terrorism and the security society inspired by it are the hermeneutic reverse side of the 500 biggest global companies and the global solidarity and concern over digital divides sponsored by them. Not only do the 'chickens come home to roost', the state terror of 'security' and of globally outsourced misery are always already linked. As Žižek (2004a, p. 185) has put it: 'More than ever, capital is the "concrete universal" of our historical epoch. What this means is that, while it remains a particular formation, it overdetermines all alternative formations, as well as all noneconomic strata of social life.' One is reminded of the Western countries that Ted Honderich (2003, pp. 110–15) calls 'hierarchical democracies': in these societies the richest 10 per cent of the population earns (and owns) thousands of times more than the lowest decile, or the poorest one-tenth of the population, and there is every reason to suppose that the wealthiest people also have more political power.

Let us think about the famous Nokia company slogan, 'Connecting People'. Here the promise of information technology lies in the conquest of isolation, the reunification of individuals. The first thing to note is how the distance communication of information societies isolates people even further. A call from a mobile may be better than no call at all, but how often does a call replace a direct contact? And is it not the distance produced by capitalism in the first place? Distance education is better than no education at all, but what if distance education replaces contact education in a situation where we are made to believe that it is too expensive? Worst of all is the belief in the pedagogical supremacy of virtual education, when, in fact, the whole trend is produced by the logic of capitalism. A connective device always also disconnects. Technology 'just works', but not in the name of a Marxian 'paradise on earth'; it works by making people work like technology in order to speed up the market and generate faster profits. Every toaster and phone is a computer; why not imagine ourselves as computers, too? But the calculative logic of presence over a distance always fails:

> We are told that, given its new way of linking and accessing information, the Internet will bring a new era of economic prosperity, lead to the development of intelligent search engines that will deliver to us just the information we desire, solve the problems of mass education, put us in touch with all of reality, allow us to have even more flexible identities ... But, compared with the relative success of e-commerce, the other areas where a new and more fulfilling form of life has been promised have produced a great deal of talk but few happy results. (Dreyfus 2001, p. 2)

The dangers of connecting people over great distances (where, why?), though great, are only part of the issue. Another question arising from the logic of symbolic capitalism is this: Who are those people who are connected by ICTs produced by telecommunication corporations? And what are their relationships? Are they the biggest economic winners of the Westernised information society? As a company, Nokia connects, for example, Asian and Finnish workers to US and Finnish owners. What kind of connections are these and what kind of information society do they represent? One side of this question is the outsourcing of jobs to China, India and other Asian countries with lower salaries, lax environmental and social laws, and rigid worker control. When the IT subcontractor Elcoteq relocated from Finland to China, it was reported that its workers in China had job contracts for a maximum of two weeks at a time. If and when the new racism of the West is characterised by economic divisions – mainly the division between Europe and Africa and Asia – it is good to pay attention to how information societies are protected from those seeking a better life. When confronted with the unfairness of its relocation from Finland to China, the CEO of Elcoteq, Antti Piippo, responded by pointing out that the company sees its global responsibility in 'Mexico, Hungary and Estonia', rather than only or mainly in Finland (Finnish News Agency, 19 March 2004). Does the responsibility of Finnish companies not lie primarily with their workers in the developing countries? And is it not, as Žižek (1998, 1999a) and others have pointed out, the workers of the First World who are sensitive over the question of foreign labour and quick to defend the borders? Should the compassion or solidarity not be shown to people who for one reason or another have left their homes? The global citizenship advocated by Hardt and Negri (2000, pp. 396–400) is a necessary consequence.

Information society 'for all' promises a lot – freedom and servitude at the same time. 'We' will be freed from fixed, formal identities locked in the structures of the old bureaucracies of nation states, from the old models of one-way broadcasting, from the supremacy of the power centres. But simultaneously this same freedom becomes a constraint: 'there is no alternative' to economic globalisation, perpetual networking, or interactivity. This form of freedom has very little to do with actual freedom; too often it is a mere facade for a very limited (formal) freedom, that is, freedom to choose from the ready-made alternatives. Furthermore, it seems as if we are already living in a time 'beyond formal freedom'. In many countries, workplace democracy is long gone, if it ever was a meaningful practice. Participation in a never-ending sequence of short-term projects is the name of the game. At the same time, economic decision-making has become ever more non-transparent, and that's why Hardt and Negri's demand for global citizenship appears to be yet another utopia. As Žižek (2004a, p. 195) reminds us, global capitalism is structurally – not only empirically – immune to representational democracy, because the decisive institutions like the IMF and the WTO do not even pretend to need representative legitimacy.

Global governance happens in different boards and councils in an *ad hoc* manner, and usually there is no democratic election to these institutions. The US uses its influence in many of these organisations, among them the G8, the World Bank, the IMF, NATO (North Atlantic Treaty Organisation), the OECD, the NAFTA (North American Free Trade Agreement), APEC (Asia-Pacific Economic Cooperation), and ASEM (Asia-Europe Meeting), which hold their meetings in gated areas or secure 'green zones' so that the effect of interactivity/passivity is perfect. It is hard to imagine a system in which we could vote for representatives in the IMF in a global ballot. The same holds true for information society theories and analysis: researchers work in a rapidly changing field with almost no firm conceptual positions, without a rigidity of authenticity and fundamental objectivity, always ready to change their viewpoint. The information society lets all the flowers bloom as long as they are information society flowers. Thus the dilemma of these theories is in their concurrent unity and diversity: The net of information theories as well as information society itself allows plurality, but in reality it acts as totality.

Surely, however, it is possible that this dilemma has been defined incorrectly? For the logic and ideas of liberalism and many single-issue social movements were founded in the same historical juncture as many of the nation states and their centralised democracies. Globalised liberal capitalism needs both the pluralistic markets in which anything can be sold *and* a universal medium: the apparently smooth regime governed by state legislation and its structural power. Maybe what is needed is a fresh universalism and more pluralism in building new life forms and new practices – a new Leviathan? Isn't it precisely this problematic dualism that catapults global capitalism to new heights as it claims to be a defender of cultural pluralism (cf. Žižek 2004a; Hardt and Negri 2000) as it also destroys that pluralism (cf. Klein 2002)?

Pluralism is something that information societies and global capital need, but it is also, according to writers like Klein, Deleuze, and Hardt and Negri, the most important form of resistance. Žižek

(2004a, p. 185) is right to criticise Klein by pointing out that when Klein attacks capitalism as a homogenising and unifying power, she criticises an old form, not the new informational capitalism. The rhizome described by Deleuze *is* the logic of digital capitalism: 'diversify, devolve power, try to mobilize local creativity and self-organisation' (ibid.). We need a sharper analysis: Žižek is right when he criticises the naive belief in revolutionary diversity, but wrong in believing that any and all diversity can be absorbed by capitalism. The plurality of the information society is the familiar plurality of brands of cereal: there is a brand for every taste but all boxes contain the same merchandise – post-gene modification, literally the same. For example, the network logic of information societies makes handicraft or subsistence-based local communities impossible, as Finnish researcher Olli Tammilehto (2003, pp. 44–5) points out:

> Local communities and poor sub-communities are integrated into the national and global economy. The prices of the products of craftsmen and small farmers drop to the world market level, which is often low simply because of the subsidies in rich countries. At the same time, the prices of raw material and farm inputs may rise because in other countries there are richer and better paying customers. This makes it impossible for the small producers to continue.

Terrorism can be commodified as 'McTerrorism', but still the existence of non-Western local communities is under threat. The choice between a Western technological lifestyle and a traditional local lifestyle is another interpassive choice: you may choose freely, as long as you pick the Western lifestyle.

The Deleuzian–Castellsian–(Žižekian?)–cybercommunist idea that the information society is somehow more 'spectral', 'malleable', 'virtual' than the previous crudely economistic societies conceals the question of what types of pluralities and local communities it favours. There is little or no evidence, for example, that the information society would not accelerate the death of languages or cultures. The levelling out and unification of local cultures may also take the form of pluralisation; indeed, the disappearance of local merchandise often happens at the same time as an explosion of different brands. At the same time, the virtual-spectral level of the networks omits the question of people: the wall separating those sheltering under the umbrella of human rights from those not so protected (Žižek 2004a) is the wall separating relative economic welfare from poverty. As Ted Honderich (2003, p. 6) points out, when we look at average life expectancy figures around the globe, 'the average lifetimes of seventy-eight and forty could suggest to someone overhearing this talk of life-times, but not knowing exactly our subject, that we are concerned with two different species'. The group of people whose human rights are 'virtual' can expect roughly a half-life, to use the term coined by Honderich, compared to rich Western people.

Is there a connection between human rights and the gap in average life spans? And does the logic of the virtual networks of the information society have something to offer when trying to understand this connection? Does the rhetoric of nodes, positions, mobility, risks, possibilities not obscure understanding by emphasising the determinative plurality of '*divide and rule*'? The free movement of information is accompanied by the ever-stricter control of the movement of people – that is, of economically excluded people. At the same time, economic inequality is becoming ever more entrenched. The situation is simple: the affluent West has to be protected simply because the late-capitalist objective of happiness-through-commodities cannot be universalised. Every place on the planet cannot become California. This is why the 'information society' is simply not a concept in the same category as 'feudalism' or 'capitalism' (Žižek 2004a, p. 193): as long as the cybercommunists and workers of immaterial production are not wholly spectral, they have to eat food and die a death. Digital technology has the potential to eliminate the scarcity of informational commodities, but this logic does not extend to the world of material goods. The interactive/passive age of the information society demands that we are ideologically and politically alert and do not mistake the loss of freedom for the proliferation of freedoms, and do '*not confuse the ruling ideology with ideology that* seems *to dominate*' (Žižek 2002a, p. 545; italics in original).

Social, Socialised, Socialist Media

As usual, the abstract promise of plurality and democratisation is supposed to be delivered by a technological innovation. In the framework of the information society, the latest buzzword is 'social media', which supposedly redeems the ills that have befallen the previous embodiments on the Internet. But, as we want to argue in the following, social media is more than social, it is socialist from the very beginning. And by this we refer not only to the end users creating and sharing content, but also to the very ways developers co-operate on the code base (building it, evaluating it, negotiating on it, and so on).

The term 'social media' can be taken to mean the on-line platforms and software people use in order to collaborate, share experiences, views, and so on, and to create their social identity. Correspondingly, 'socialised media' would mean, in this context, such tools when they are owned, maintained and managed by the community of users itself. Examples of this kind of self-management proliferate in the hacker community. There are even cases of actively socialising previously private media. For example, hackers have collected money to purchase the source code of computer programs in order to develop them freely and to release them from the commodified world. The most famous example of this kind of commercial 'socialisation' is the 3D animation software Blender (see http://en.wikipedia. org/wiki/Blender_%28software%29) that was acquired in 2002 from the company that originally developed the software, and has continued as an open-source project maintained by the Blender Foundation (the sum of €100,000 was collected in seven weeks; now Blender code is released under the copyleft GNU General Public Licence). The Wikipedia itself has financed its server park and small staff through fundraising from its users.

But are these means enough in facilitating peoples' skills and opportunities to participate in the digitalised world, to be in dialogue with each other by using social media? And, more importantly, are these means themselves digital? Žižek (2002a, p. 544) argues, convincingly, that dialogue, both in its traditional forms and in the form of social media, takes us only to the gates of authentic and substantial democracy, or what Žižek, after Lenin, refers to as 'actual freedom' which undermines the very co-ordinates of existing power relations. Maybe we need to take the hacker ideology of Free/Libre Open Source Software (FLOSS) to its next logical step, that of 'socialist media', where 'socialist' refers to shared ownership, use and administration of a given media as much as to a certain mindset of collaborative learning, solidarity and sharing. As Žižek (2002b) puts it in his view of 'cybercommunism':

> Is there not also an explosive potential for capitalism itself in the world wide web? Is not the lesson of the Microsoft monopoly precisely the Leninist one: instead of fighting its monopoly through the state apparatus (recall the court-ordered split of the Microsoft corporation), would it not be more 'logical' just to socialize it, rendering it freely accessible? Today one is thus tempted to paraphrase Lenin's well-known motto, 'Socialism = electrification + the power of the soviets': 'Socialism = free access to internet + the power of the soviets.'

As the true believers of new technologies claim, echoing the old axiom of technological determinism, anything that can be presented as digital code, as a series of ones and zeros, can and will be copied at very little cost and no loss to the original. After the needed infrastructure is in place, digital information is not a scarce resource any more. Consequently, a cornucopian digital economy supposedly transcends the physical limitations of traditional economies.

Correspondingly, on the social level the digital world has been seen as the first seed of new forms of organisation that will have radical political effects. Volunteer hacker organisations and the various civil society activities organised with the help of the Internet have been seen, on the one hand, as providing fresh blood for the Habermasian ideal of democratic communication and, on the other hand, as completely new forms of civic self-organisation and self-management (for theories on hacker communities, see Castells 1996; Himanen 2000). For instance, while looking for examples of the new multitudes that they advocate as the basic self-organising models of future politics, Michael Hardt and Antonio Negri (2004, p. 301) turn to free and open-source software communities and related activities. When the self-organisational nature of hacker communities is combined with the observation that digital code is not a scarce resource, we approach a cybercommunist utopia where volunteer organisations and communities of non-alienated labour manage themselves in a post-scarcity economy (see, for example, Žižek 2002b, 2006b; Merten 2000).

One of the crucial consequences of digitalisation has to do with the very conditions of material capitalist economy if compared to the 'second economy' brought forth by the digital sphere. A whole school of writers (for an overview, see Lessig 2006) has argued that, in addition to the capitalist economy, there exists another economy, variously called, for example, 'amateur economy', 'sharing economy', 'social production economy', 'non-commercial economy', 'participatory economy', 'p2p economy', or even 'gift economy'. The problem these thinkers want to emphasise is that the 'second economy' works with its own principles and that an attempt to force it into the mode of the capitalist economy cannot be sustained and would be disastrous to the ideology of FLOSS.

Is the sometimes violent process of socialising the answer? Would it be better if we could take another logical step – a quantum leap or, perhaps, a leap of faith – from there, and start from the outset to talk about and invent what we would like to call – just for the sake of it – socialist media, instead of social, and socialised media? What would the world be like if there were exemplars of socialist media? And what would those exemplars be like? Can we thus consider the Wikipedia an example of socialist media? Do we have other examples? To answer this question, we need to answer another question: What are the definitive characteristics of a socialist media?

Technical and Political Conditions

Besides the obvious technological infrastructure (servers, computers, and other devices) needed to organise and use social media, energy (electricity, food) is as vital. But the crucial question is: who owns and provides energy? An answer to this basic question takes us from the digital realm to the realm of material production, and to the core of critical political economy.

The sad fact is that most energy resources are owned by private international corporations. They are in many ways key players in the arena of international politics, directing foreign policy, and making decisions about war and peace. But there is another way of thinking about the ownership of resources such as energy. It is called 'common wealth'. The term comes from the Latin *res publica*, meaning 'common things' and, by extension, 'a democratic republic'. In the theory of critical political economy, energy is considered to be a central part of common wealth, which should not be owned by profit-making private companies, but by the state and the people. Unfortunately or not, this is the definitive precondition for social media ever to be a truly revolutionary force. Thus, in this sense, 'social' and 'political' still rule the 'digital', for, imitating Žižek's 'Leninist' formula, free access to the Internet still demands an electricity supply.

This demand assumes quite straightforwardly that the state and the people take back their common wealth from the global players. Without this logical step, open access is freedom without freedom. Without public ownership of material resources, the ideology of FLOSS remains another one-issue social movement without an authentic political aspect. But quite the reverse has been happening: 'A substantial part of the Russian electricity sector created by Lenin to modernise the new Soviet economy is to be privatised with a series of floats expected on the London stock exchange', reported the *Guardian* in July 2006 (Macalister 2006). Lenin saw electricity and oil as key aspects of global imperial capitalism, and tried to make a case against these imperial powers and their bourgeois defenders, which acted as cartels and monopolies. In his *Imperialism, the Highest Stage of Capitalism* (1916), Lenin stated that certain reactionary writers

> have expressed the opinion that international cartels, being one of the most striking expressions of the internationalisation of capital, give the hope of peace among nations under capitalism. Theoretically, this opinion

is absolutely absurd, while in practice it is sophistry and a dishonest defense of the worst opportunism. International cartels show to what point capitalist monopolies have developed, and the object of the struggle between the various capitalist associations. This last circumstance is the most important; it alone shows us the historico-economic meaning of what is taking place; for the forms of the struggle may and do constantly change in accordance with varying, relatively specific and temporary causes, but the substance of the struggle, its class content, positively cannot change while classes exist.

That said, we must of course emphasise the contradiction between a Leninist point of view – a vanguard party leading the masses – and the obvious fact that in the Wikiworld there is no centre, and no vanguards controlling digital development. This contradiction contains another one, that between the ownership of natural resources by states or corporations, and the intellectual resources of the people. Contrary to the Leninist idea, the key to emancipation in the sphere of social media and its socio-political consequences could be 'oscillation and plurality ... in the plurality and complexity of "voices": an emancipation consisting in dis-orientation which is, at the same time, a liberation of dialect, local differences, and rationalities, each with its own distinctive grammar and syntax' (Peters and Lankshear 1996, p. 60).

But we must add that simultaneously there may be some glimpse of hope in developments pointing away from the internationalisa-tion of capital. As an example, let us consider the case of Venezuela and its 'Bolivarian revolution', and a new trend to nationalise natural resources. Venezuela not only has substantial natural resources of oil, but also has the political leadership and will to use those resources for the peoples' well being, and not for the benefit of foreign investors. The same holds true in other Latin American countries such as Chile and Bolivia. In this instance it is worth mentioning that the government of Venezuela have launched their own 'Bolivarian computers' with free Linux operating system; President Chávez's aim is to 'promote technological development' and help 'reach technological independence' (Carlson 2007). Similarly, in Brazil the cultural ministry headed by Gilberto Gil has started domestic programs promoting free software and the Creative Commons copyright platform. Internationally, Brazil has been one of the leading countries working for a global copyright regime that would not be systematically geared against the countries in the southern hemisphere. The most important issues have to do with medical patents, but – right or wrong – the fate of copyright for computer software is often decided in the same organisations (such as WIPO).

And speaking of the República Bolivariana de Venezuela, the Bolivarian Republic of Venezuela, President Chávez has chosen a totally different route to other former social democracies such as Finland and Sweden, where previously state-owned companies in energy, transportation and postal services have been privatised and taken to the world market via the stock exchange. As Žižek has put it in comparing Venezuela with the reformist, 'third way' left, and Subcomandante Marcos in Chiapas, Mexico (and at the same time covertly criticising John Holloway's 2005 book, *Change the World Without Taking Power*):

It is striking that the course on which Hugo Chávez has embarked since 2006 is the exact opposite of the one chosen by the postmodern Left: far from resisting state power, he grabbed it (first by an attempted coup, then democratically), ruthlessly using the Venezuelan state apparatuses to promote his goals. Furthermore, he is militarising the barrios, and organising the training of armed units there. And, the ultimate scare: now that he is feeling the economic effects of capital's 'resistance' to his rule (temporary shortages of some goods in the state-subsidised supermarkets), he has announced plans to consolidate the 24 parties that support him into a single party. Even some of his allies are sceptical about this move: will it come at the expense of the popular movements that have given the Venezuelan revolution its élan? However, this choice, though risky, should be fully endorsed: the task is to make the new party function not as a typical state socialist (or Peronist) party, but as a vehicle for the mobilisation of new forms of politics (like the grass roots slum committees). What should we say to someone like Chávez? 'No, do not grab state power, just withdraw, leave the state and the current situation in place'? Chávez is often dismissed as a clown – but wouldn't such a withdrawal just reduce him to a version of Subcomandante Marcos, whom many Mexican leftists now refer to as 'Subcomediante Marcos'? Today, it is the great capitalists – Bill Gates, corporate polluters, fox hunters – who 'resist' the state. The lesson here is that the truly subversive thing is not to insist on 'infinite' demands we know those in power cannot fulfil. Since they know that we know it, such an 'infinitely demanding' attitude presents no problem for those in power: 'So wonderful that, with your critical demands, you remind us what kind of world we would all like to live in. Unfortunately, we live in the real world, where we have to make do with what is possible.' The thing to do is, on the contrary, to bombard those in power with strategically well-selected, precise, finite demands, which can't be met with the same excuse. (Žižek 2007a)

Social and Individual Conditions

The physical energy – electricity – needed for running social media sites is one condition. Another is the less tangible energy and time needed in order for individuals to contribute. For instance, the crown jewel of FLOSS, the GNU/Linux operating system, still receives more contributions of new code from the US and Europe than anywhere else. This bias, which can be seen in many major open collaboration projects, including the Wikipedia, should direct our attention to the different possibilities that present themselves to individuals in different geopolitical and socio-economic settings. The fact that cases like Blender and the Wikipedia depend on substantial donations points to the importance of relative affluence.

Linus Torvalds, the inventor of the Linux operating system, was a student at the University of Helsinki (Finland) when the Linux project began, and a beneficiary of the Finnish welfare state, including tuition-free access to the university and its resources, such as computer labs. In addition, the Linux code was initially hosted by the Finnish University Network (FUNET). All of this suggests the fact that non-alienated knowledge work on the Internet does seem to need a certain basis of affluence and public educational and social infrastructure (sometimes referred to as safety nets) before it can take off. However, it seems that competences built by individuals in a free and public educational system will often primarily benefit corporations like the mobile phone company Nokia, and not the public sector. Even so, these economic mega-players, exploiting the workforce and the state, dare to claim that the state does not support their business enough in terms of radical tax cuts. What is needed is a counter-move to free people's minds and intellectual resources from the slavery of the corporation as well as from the slavery of the state and its marketised educational system.

Nordic countries already enjoy many cultural and social characteristics which allow counter-moves and actual freedoms. These include a progressive taxation-supported schooling system from kindergarten to higher education, libraries, cultural institutions such as museums, and so on. Indeed, the step from a social media constrained by liberal communism to socialist media needs not only basic welfare but also actual control of life goals and non-physical needs. Paradoxically or not, the road to the latter runs through the collective or common control of the production of basic welfare (including things like electricity and access to the Internet). In addition, such welfare strategies or innovations as a social wage, citizenship income, or unconditional basic income would pave the way to the socialist media, and structurally enhanced universal well being. Thus, for us, socialist media refers to two core things, one ideological-pedagogical and one economical-material, if you wish: on the one hand, free speech, everyone can – and must! – participate, for everyone knows everything; and, on the other hand, common ownership (including not only content and code, but also material resources and the physical energy to run the mill).

Or, as Hardt and Negri put it in their *Empire* (2000, p. 403):

The demand for a social wage extends to the entire population the demand that all activity necessary for the production of capital be recognized with an equal compensation such that a social wage is really a guaranteed income. Once citizenship is extended to all, we could call this guaranteed income a citizenship income, due to each as a member of society.

Educationally speaking, an entirely new social mentality and an ideology of shared ownership are needed. In many schools, children are taught to do their own work, not to collaborate or to use pre-existing materials as they learn. An urgent task for critical educators is to strengthen a sense of community and solidarity as well as an interest in different points of view. In this sense, socialist media have a revolutionary potential for increasing global understanding of difference and overcoming the capitalist drift towards global commodification.

There are several expressions of different forms of socialism, as Peters reminds us. They 'revolve around the international labour movement and invoke new imperialism struggles based on the movements of indigenous and racialised peoples' (Peters 2004). A starting point for the social condition of socialist media could be built around the concept of 'knowledge socialism'. This refers to the politics of knowledge, on the one hand, to intellectual property rights and intellectual resources in general, including questions of expert versus amateur knowledge as explicated by Peters, on the other hand (2004):

> In these discussions, issues of freedom and control reassert themselves at all levels: at those of content, code and information. This issue of freedom/control concerns the ideation and codification of knowledge and the new 'soft' technologies that take the notion of 'practice' as the new desideratum: practitioner knowledge, communities of practice, and different forms of organisational learning adopted and adapted as part of corporate practice. Indeed, now we face the politics of the learning economy and the economics of forgetting that insists new ideas have only a short shelf life. ... These questions are also tied up with larger questions concerning disciplinary versus informal knowledge, the formalisation of the disciplines, the development of the informal knowledge economy, and the pervasiveness of informal education. Informal knowledge and education based on free exchange is still a good model for civil society in the age of knowledge capitalism.

In building socialist or participatory media, a presumption that the mode of production shapes the context in which psychological and social processes take place, and consciousness is formed, should be taken into account (Youngman 1986, p. 101). Thus the revolutionary potential of wikis. In the first place, the Wikipedia, or any other form of wiki, is not a technology but praxis, a collective activity. It involves purpose and intention, and in this sense, 'knowledge arises and deepens within a continuous process of activity, conceptualisation, and renewed activity' (ibid., p. 96). As knowledge can be defined in this instance as a social product, it always involves hegemonic battles over the power to rule and regulate. In a capitalist society, the ruling elite owns the media and thus sets the dominant agenda. But inside this capitalist realm, the Wikiworld is evolving as yet another hegemonic battleground marking the turning of the tide, for in the Wikiworld people have unprecedented powers.

The Wikiworld is not only a counter-hegemonic move but a serious, hard-to-stop mass activity. The Wikipedia, and other wikis, are lived, educationally-laden social situations. If 'hegemony is the result of lived social relationships and not simply the dominance of ideas, then the experiences inherent in educational situations (i.e. the totality of knowledge, attitudes, values and relationships) is as significant as the purely intellectual content' (ibid., p. 105). In other words, the mere process of being in and part of the development of the Wikipedia and the like is a critical learning experience towards the birth of socialist media and the embodiment of Marx's (1858) concept of general intellect.

> The development of fixed capital indicates to what degree general social knowledge has become a direct force of production, and to what degree, hence, the conditions of the process of social life itself have come under the control of the general intellect and been transformed in accordance with it. To what degree the powers of social production have been produced, not only in the form of knowledge, but also as immediate organs of social practice, of the real life process.

Based on a close textual reading – 'short-circuiting' – of Lenin, Žižek refers to the idea of general intellect as a huge 'accounting apparatus' without which, says Lenin, socialism is impossible. In the words of Lenin, to make socialism happen is to make this massive apparatus 'even bigger, even more democratic, even more comprehensive. … This will be country-wide book-keeping, country-wide accounting of the production and distribution of goods, this will be, so to speak, something in the nature of the skeleton of socialist society' (Žižek 2006a). To Žižek this marks 'the most radical expression of Marx's notion of the general intellect regulating all social life in a transparent way, of the post-political world in which "administration of people" is supplanted by the "administration of things"'. Žižek further notes that it is easy to criticise Lenin by referring to the horrors of the real socialist experiment in the Soviet Union, especially Stalin's era, and the apparatus of social administrations which grow 'even bigger'. But as Žižek asks: 'Are, however, things really so unambiguous? What if one replaces the (obviously dated) example of the central bank with the World Wide Web, today's perfect candidate for the General Intellect?' (ibid.) What, indeed, if one replaces the example of the World Wide Web with the Wikiworld, including the servers and the power plants?

As Kellner (2004) writes, the key question is not a moralistic one – whether social media are good or bad in the hands of critical educators. Rather, it is a question of what critical educators can do with Wikipedia and other forms of social media in helping to create 'a more democratic and egalitarian society and what their limitations are for producing more active and creative human beings and a more just society'.

It goes without saying that the Wikipedia and other wikis can be used in formal education. But there is a certain tardiness and conservatism in the educational system. This holds true throughout the whole system, all the way from the public sphere to the corridors of the Ministry of Education and to the privacy of a single classroom. In some countries, like Finland, the state has for years promoted the use of computers and new information and computer literacies and skills, but as soon as the goals have been identified and campaigns have begun, the technologies and skills needed have already changed several times. The system logic or the grip of the state educational apparatus does not hold in the Wikiworld. In many Western countries, not to mention some authoritarian regimes, the state has used technocratic rationality to try to regulate the digital sphere educationally. It has acted as if it did not want people to liberate themselves in the area of digital literacy. Therefore, as Kellner and Kahn (2006) have stated in their critique of technoliteracy ruled from above, there must be another way:

> We cannot stress it enough: the project of reconstructing technoliteracy must take different forms in different contexts. In almost every cultural and social situation, however, a literacy of critique should be enhanced so that citizens can name the technological system, describe and grasp the technological changes occurring as defining features of the new global order, and learn to experimentally engage in critical and oppositional practices in the interests of democratization and progressive transformation. As part of a truly multicultural order, we need to encourage the growth and flourishing of numerous standpoints ... on technoliteracy, looking out for and legitimizing counter-hegemonic needs, values, and understandings. Such would be to propound multiple technoliteracies 'from below' as opposed to the largely functional, economistic, and technocratic technoliteracy 'from above' that is favoured by many industries and states.

This emphasis on the perspective 'from below' reminds us of the end of Marx's Volume One of *Capital*, and the unhappy Mr Peel. As Francis Wheen (2006) put it, Marx's most remarkable anecdote in the last pages is about this Mr Peel, who moved from England to Australia along with £50,000 and 3,000 workers, but didn't take into account the fact that while he could carry with him 'property in money, means of subsistence, machines, and other means of production', he could not take the wage worker who was ready to sell him- or herself of his or her own free will. In Marx's words, Mr Peel didn't understand that 'capital is not a thing, but a social relation between persons' (Marx 1867). Thus, writes Marx: 'Unhappy Mr. Peel who provided for everything except the export of English modes of production to Swan River!' (ibid.). Just as the wage workers discovered the freedom in the seemingly boundless land of Western Australia to build their own lives, we are now witnessing more and more people discovering their freedom in the borderlands of information technologies, given that they do not fall into a corporate trap, that is, that they not only acknowledge business interests and new modes in capitalist commodification around social media (that is, technology firms' aim to use consumers and users as co-creators of their products), but that they are also able to detach capitalist tendencies from authentic voluntary work, work for fun or work just for the sake of it.

Let us summarise here the essential principles of a socialist media in the Wikiworld using the ideals of Project Oekonux, an inspiring German co-operative effort for theorising and furthering the economic and political forms of FLOSS (see http://www. oekonux.org/). These are the absence of alienation which results from the direct needs of those involved; self-organisation; and voluntary participation, including the voluntary assumption of responsibility, or *Selbstentfaltung* in the project's terminology (as responsibility and autonomy-in-interdependence). Here, freedom has a triple meaning: freedom is the result of the process, a precondition of the process, and enables the freedom of others (http://en.wiki.oekonux.org/Oekonux/Introduction/). In our view, these principles sound like socialism or 'cybercommunism'.

It is, of course, always a threat that the promise of evolving socialist principles in the Wikiworld will be reduced to such banalities as 'If it's not fun, why do it?' (as the corny motto of some Linux people goes). While this might well motivate people in the affluent world, in a Žižekian tone we could counter that this principle is for nerds and consumerists only: there is nothing 'fun' in the Wikiworld if it is created for real reasons and real aims, that is, if its purpose is to pave the way for overcoming the gritty realities of capitalist forms of production. But is it reasonable to believe that people in the West are aware of all the problems capitalism is creating? Is it reasonable to think that there could be an overall wake-up call for economical, social and individual change in the current context of spin, when advertising, manipulation and the manufacturing of consent are so widespread?

Besides the growing use of FLOSS-based ICTs there are at least two tendencies that increase hope for a fairer world. One is the now evident fact of climate change, which compels us to re-evaluate our consumption habits and overuse of natural resources.

The twin of climate change is the growing awareness of ecological limits: the depletion of fossil fuels, mainly oil. Together these two sides of the coin will force a change, whether we want it or not. The other is what Andre Gorz terms as the lost magic of the work- or wage-based society (Gorz 1999). In modern times, Taylorist work failed to deliver enough social coherence, but instead created abstract and weak social bonds between people. The basic idea behind the construction of socialist media is the people's need for a personal and mutually shared narrative, for a mental and emotional anchor that helps them gain respect and a sense of solidarity in a situation where working life deprives people of continuity and long-term planning. In short, what we need is a culture (Sennett 2006, p. 183), a common culture, and in that respect socialist media is a means to achieve that vital goal.

New rules for the use of energy and consumer habits along with the use of social media in its socialist form can at their best make a great change not only in people's minds and behaviour but also in the very forms of production. So, in sum, we get the equation 'socialist media = basic welfare + common servers + the power of the soviets'. Basic welfare and common servers provide the material basis, while the 'power of the soviets' refers to the ideological component of radical universalism: everyone already is the master of his or her own knowledge, learning and being. Here we echo the old Marxian idea that the soviet, as a collective of production and wisdom, is the dialectical basis for individuation and personal freedom. Of course, the order of the ingredients or the components in the formula can be different; in other words, there can be different orders of the free and open world without scarcity (that is, basic welfare = electricity + the power of the soviets + socialist media).

Freedom, More Freedom!

An alternative way of conceptualising the transition from social to socialist media is to think about the freedoms involved. The read-only culture proposed by ultra-commoditised and mechanised lifestyles can be seen from the perspective of both media and education. In one extreme, a totalitarian state, like Plato's utopia in *The Republic*, will want to control education, reserving true knowledge for the philosopher-kings and telling a 'royal lie' to the working classes in order to keep them at bay. As a citizen of Athens, Plato would have known exactly why the movement calling for the abolition of copyrights is called the 'Pirate Party' (for instance, in Sweden: http://www.piratpartiet.se). The Platonist closed-source approach is strictly correlative with media as a private profit-making business where information first and foremost has an exchange value.

As we move toward freer modes of media and education, we first encounter social media and education as entrepreneurship, where the subjects are 'empowered' by active participation in economically constrained activities. This is the first order of freedom, where you have free speech within the confines of formal freedom (as explained by Žižek 2004c): you are free in so far as you do not rock the boat. Formal freedom is just not enough, as Eric Weiner plainly states in the following quote:

> It is not enough to be free to speak, if those who are speaking do not have the power to create the conditions in which they can be heard. Likewise, it is not adequate to be free to choose if the choice about what choices can be made has already been made by someone else. This level of freedom is for suckers; it is for those who choose unquestionably between Coke and Pepsi, but never think about who decides what goes into the machine. (Weiner 2007, p. 260)

The ultimate question is, What goes into the machine where 'machine' refers to the logic of a formally free market, free choice and capitalism itself? Strangely enough, the road to more freedom involves the realisation that the economic constraints of liberal, multicultural capitalism are not nearly strict enough. Only when the ghost of exchange value is stripped away is the persistent and non-symbolic use value, or value in itself, revealed. In terms of media, this means Linux or the Wikipedia, which do not have any exchange value but have a tremendous utility. But even that is not enough in terms of taking economics seriously: the *oikos* (the greek word for 'household' at the root of our term 'economy') that humanity is facing, is the planet and its finite resources as a whole, not the impoverishing economics of gross domestic product and the Dow Jones index. Native skills (education) and indigenous information need a sustainable material lifestyle, which is something the West has not been able to devise so far. Neither has it been able to eliminate the old traces of triple-freedom (see Table 6.1), or the semi-paradoxical seeds of triple-freedom inside civilisation itself.

Thus the last two modes of freedom are linked to the emergence of changes in the modes of production, governance and property. These changes will occur through the following three processes. They will 'produce use-value through the free cooperation of producers who have access to distributed capital' (distributed intellectual resources, computer networks, pooled finance): this is what is called 'the p2p production mode', or a 'third mode of production' which differs from the capitalist 'anything-for-profit standard', or from public production by state-owned enterprises common to welfare states. The product and purpose of the p2p production mode is not to produce useless commodities or 'exchange value for a market, but use-value for a community of users'. The changes will also be 'governed by the community of producers themselves, and not by market allocation or corporate hierarchy: this is the p2p governance mode, or third mode of governance'. In addition, they 'make use-value freely accessible on a universal basis, through new common property regimes. This is its distribution or "peer property mode": a "third mode of ownership," different from private property or public (state) property' (Bauwens 2005).

The last two modes of freedom in particular bring us to the fundamental epistemological changes in how future generations will cope with the world. The first has to do with *radical openness* in the very media people use. It allows or demands that people participate and collaborate with each other. And it also allows them to see how knowledge is constructed – as in the Wikipedia and other wikis – where creation and negotiation can be tracked very precisely by clicking the 'history' and 'discussion' buttons.

Table 6.1   Levels of Freedom

	Characteristics	*Media*	*Education*
Closed	Exchange value	Media as corporate business	Education as an ideological state apparatus
	Vehicle and content controlled	Economic utility, control of content (business logic)	Economic utility, control of content (educational policy)
	Commoditisation		Learning as having
	'Crowdsourcing'		Prolonged exchange value of well-educated citizens
First stage of freedom	Economical utility, limited collaboration	Web 2.0	Educational content business
	Market sphere, entrepreneurship, multicultural capitalism, liberal communism	YouTube, Google, CitizenTV, Adbusters, Yahoo Answers, Knol ...	Teachers and students as commodified semi-objects (knowledge creators, consumers)
	Limited autonomy of content		
	'Sharing'	'Produsers'	
Double-Free	Use value/value in itself	Media as collaboration	Education as collaboration
	Full autonomy of content, limited autonomy of vehicle	Wikis, Linux, p2p	Freire, *Selbstentfaltung*
	'Commonist'	'Access to the Internet + power of the soviets'	Learning as being
			Reflective uncertainty
Triple-free	Value inseparable from the world, Aristotelian finalities	Immediate media practices	'Deschooling societies'
	Full autonomy of content and vehicle	Wikipedia + ecological autonomy + control of resources	Learning by doing, native skills
		The Pirate Bay (?), Tolstoy Farm and *Indian Opinion*	
	Promoting other than materially-driven life forms		Students and teachers as human beings, 'lifelong learners' in an existential sense
	'Communist'	'Electricity + access to the Internet + power of the soviets'	Education as commons

The Pirate Bay (http://thepiratebay.org) file-sharing site has been a promising candidate for triple-freedom. The site has been dedicated to serve as a knot – or a safe haven if you like – for free downloads of audio-visual materials including otherwise commercial contents, but they also own their own servers (not the electricity, however). In 2007, there was a brief attempt by the Pirates to buy a small island in order to form an independent nation of their own. This would have been an exhilarating step toward triple-freedom, and the need to take the step is ever present.

The only pure example of a triple-free immediate media practice we can think of is the Tolstoy Farm run by Gandhi and his collaborators in South Africa. From 1910, the farm, a kind of ashram, was run on the principle of self-subsistence and self-reliance (see Bhana 1975). The participants all worked the land, growing vegetables, and took part in writing and printing the newspaper *Indian Opinion* that was delivered by train to Johannesburg. There was also a school on the farm in which the children were taught both 'mental' and 'manual' skills, including the making of their own clothes and footwear. In the paper, Gandhi and his fellow *satyagrahi* continued the struggle for justice and equality. In this sense, the *Indian Opinion* was not only a newspaper among others, but one of the embodiments of the Tolstoy Farm as a collective, like its gardens and workshops.

The second change, that of *reflective uncertainty*, is linked to the ability to track the changes made in wikis and other collaborative sites. The ability to track changes leads to a world in which people begin to take for granted that many areas of human conduct and knowledge are based on processes of negotiation and meaning-making both in virtual spaces and elsewhere. And perhaps more than that, they will eventually decide to become ever more responsible for the world, as agents of history, by abolishing the distinctions between those who know and do, and those who consume and obey. They will question the pedagogical myth 'that there is an inferior intelligence and a superior one' (Rancière 1991, p. 7). Therefore a teaching and learning method suited to the Wikiworld 'is above all the universal verification of the similarity of what all the emancipated can do, all those who have decided to think of themselves as people just like everyone else' (ibid., p. 41).

In the realm of the Internet, or the Wikiworld, collaborative, peer-to-peer practices are flourishing. These practices utilise people's 'general intellect', common knowledge and voluntary participation. Criteria of the emancipatory teaching and learning method will become fully operational after an open access principle and free software applications are combined with free and open studies and education in places like the Wikiversity on the Internet, or free universities and other free learning associations. For, in these evolving worlds of free studies, an interest is not in the 'potential capability' or talent but in everyone's ability to participate and learn equally, to take according to one's needs and to give according to one's abilities. This way, the promises of equal education are also redeemed as universal human rights. At best, collaborative practices in the Wikiworld present new forms of internationalism, common will and the power of the people. *If we want, we can!* Rancière sheds light on his own idea as follows:

> From my point of view, the Internet is similar to what writing was at a certain moment. It meant the circulation of words and knowledge which could be appropriated by anyone. It is not a question of giving knowledge to everybody, it is a question of having words circulate in a free and desirable way, and I think that this is what's happening with the Internet. That is probably why some reactionary people are so angry with the Internet, saying it's horrible that people log on to the web and they can find everything they want, that it is against research and intelligence. I would say no, it is the way intelligence, equal intelligence, works. You wander randomly in a library the same way you surf randomly on the Internet. This is, from my point of view, what equality of intelligence means. (Lie and Rancière 2006)

Rancière's idea seems to be that education and learning are a means of participating in politics, or more precisely, they are forms of political socialisation; the way education is arranged has significant political and social consequences. Methods and forms of education can be used either to support the system or to change it. In the modern nation states overall political goals in social and economic policy also determine the aims of education. Emancipatory education is not a suitable training system for the modern state, but points to the possibility of a totally different social order; and maybe also to the need for an altogether different world.

Where some theorists of critical education are unconvinced that critical educational practices can help to change the world (see Holst 2002, pp. 78–9), Rancière answers the question affirmatively. From his point of view, furthermore, the question has been incorrectly put, since education, society and politics are always inseparable; they are intertwined, or woven into each other. The question is only how they and their complex, ideological and hegemonic relations are defined. For Rancière, the emancipatory practice of education is the birthplace of radically equal society. It fulfils the following principles: *You can do what you want to do, and as a teacher you should teach what you don't know – and learn what you want to learn!*

In this respect, a defining character of the Wikiworld is its radical openness and anti-Cartesian uncertainty. The reliability of Wikipedia is dependent on us; that is, it is not only dependent on you or me as individuals, but on us as the community comprising the various skills and literacies that we share as members of that community. The difference is clear when compared with printed media, which in this sense is closed and relies on gated and copyrighted communities of expertise for authority. Correspondingly, the idea of reflective uncertainty has a family resemblance to the 'learning as participation' metaphor that emphasises participation in various cultural practices and shared learning activities (in kindergarten, at school, at university and in various informal learning sites, workplaces and organisational activities). In this metaphor, knowledge and learning are situated and created in people's everyday lives, or their lifeworlds, and as part of their socio-cultural context which existentially includes the material means of subsistence or production.

In his *Economic and Philosophic Manuscripts* of 1844, Marx writes:

> The alienation of the worker in his product means not only that his labour
> becomes an object, an external existence, but that it exists outside him,
> independently, as something alien to him, and that it becomes a power on
> its own confronting him. It means that the life which he has conferred on the
> object confronts him as something hostile and alien. (Marx 1844, p. 272)

Marx speaks to critical wiki educators in as much as they feel obliged to facilitate themselves and their fellow learners to overcome their alienation. In the context of the Wikiworld, this task can be approached and conceptualised as a distinction between 'making' and 'made'. The latter refers to alienated work and learning that is already made, that is, its parameters are set in advance, and the worker has no power over its rules and regulations. Not only must he or she take these limitations for granted, but they also tear away from the acting subject the object he or she has produced (a piece of software, a piece of educational material, and so on); whereas in the 'doing format' – the non-alienated, or free learning – the acting subject cannot only learn and produce free, but is also willing to share his or her products and results of learning with others without granting the right to commercial hoarding (this is why copyleft is crucial); in other words, products of learning are always in the process of making, and becoming something.

Let us think of a Wikipedia article. In terms of the division between 'making' and 'made' a wiki text represents an open possibility of joining forces and learning together via the mediation of the wiki page. This is what is meant by non-alienated making, creating and doing together. The same goes with classroom learning, in which a competent teacher uses various learning materials from the readymade (done, alienated) textbooks to the Internet, not to speak of the unfolding dialogue in the room. And in the best possible world a competent teacher can make her own teaching materials by using the wonders of the Wikiworld along with other learners, and thus is able to wikify his or her own teaching practice.

From our point of view, the beauty of social media such as the Wikipedia is precisely in the p2p use value based on collective anonymous contributions (and everyone's right not to contribute and still use common resources). For us, the triple-freedom of social media means *anonymous collectivism*. In this respect Google's competitor to the Wikipedia known as Knol (http:// knol.google.com) does not fulfil the triple-free standard of social media, but stays somewhere in between closed and first stage of freedom in terms of openness and collectivism.

Knol, a Unit of Knowledge

Knol is Google's counteraction to the Wikipedia in building 'units of knowledge'. Knol consist of authoritative articles about specific topics. Authority is based on a writer's ownership: 'A knol "owner" is a person associated with the knol who has control over administrative settings for the knol, like copyright licensing options, collaboration models.' The owner then decides and specifies the level of collaboration she wants with the larger community. In the Knol web site the following word of caution is given – rather hilariously from the point of view of Wikiworld's basic premises of sharing, collaboration and trust: 'Remember that by extending ownership of the knol to another person, you are giving them responsibility for administering the knol and the ability to control those settings. A co-owner can do anything with a knol, including removing you as an owner, deleting the knol, changing its license or collaboration model, or changing who receives AdSense revenue from ads appearing on the knol. So be careful, only give ownership to persons you know and trust.'
(http://knol.google.com/k/)

Compared to the Wikipedia's *anonymous collectivism*, Knol promotes *personified individualism*, individual authorship and individual control in deciding who is able to participate and contribute. Thus it builds its ideology mainly on a closed model, and keeps the door open for exchange value and knowledge business. Even the subtitle of Knol is rather telling: every contribution is 'a unit of knowledge', a separated universe controlled by an individualised author; Knol celebrates alienated individuality by forming a gated or altogether closed community, an expert being a hero of his or her own knowledge creation. This ignores the social history of knowledge which, even in its Western guise, is a story of collective thinking and wisdom.

Thus the Wikipedia is closer to the standard interpretation of how innovations and new ideas are born: those who develop intellectual pursuits and search for truth always stand on the shoulders of giants past and present. In fact, the two extremes of the Wikipedia and Knol embody two types of sociality: the Wikipedia builds on the principle of radical inclusiveness – giving voice to everyone regardless of class, age, gender, ethnicity, religion, and so on – whereas Knol is more of an exclusive site for learning.

CONCLUSION, OR TOWARDS EDUCATIONAL SUPERABUNDANCE

Where, then, are the promises of a new order of learning, free from the constraints of capitalism and state-governed formal learning? Where should we look for the forces to change the social order of pre-regulated, alienating learning? Not perhaps from the demolition or state-regulated reform of formal schooling, and not perhaps from an increase of precisely tuned, monitored and just-in-time delivered utilitarian education. The answer *does* lie in learning more, but in the sense of learning and being for the sake of learning and being themselves. This is what we mean by educational superabundance living not only on the internal crisis-ridden development of capitalism but also in the dark gaps of the market mechanism. Rancière points precisely to these apparently useless modes of learning:

> A worker [a learner, a teacher, a student ...] who had never learned how to write and yet tried to compose verses to suit the taste of his times was perhaps more of a danger to the prevailing ideological order than a worker who performed revolutionary songs. ... Perhaps the truly dangerous classes are not so much the uncivilised ones thought to undermine society from below, but rather the migrants who move at the borders between classes, individuals and groups who develop capabilities within themselves which are useless for the improvement of their material lives and which in fact are liable to make them despise material concerns. (Rancière 1988, p. 50)

Of course, we are reading these words both literally and metaphorically. In the latter sense those migrants 'who move at the borders between classes' can be thought of as young people especially who often face the new technology point-blank and as foot soldiers of the digital age who learn wiki practices from their peers, rather than from the formal schooling system. In the literal sense, Wikiworld is a site for learning in which individuals and groups really 'develop capabilities within themselves which are useless for the improvement of their material lives and which in fact are liable to make them despise material concerns' as hackers have done before, and as we, ordinary people, are increasingly learning to do.

For Rancière, universality is the starting point of the process, not the end point. We should act on the basis that everyone is already equal, not only or mainly on the premise that in the end everyone will be made equal. This characterises socialist media. The perfect illustration is the premise on which the radical openness of the Wikipedia editorial process is based: in terms of knowledge, we are all already equal, which is why everyone is free to contribute. We need not wait until the results of a complicated educational process are finished before we can be confident that everyone 'has' knowledge or 'expertise'. The same principle of starting from universality can be applied in other situations. Think of an EU immigration officer facing a group of people arrived from Africa on a makeshift boat. The officer should proceed from the authentically universalist premise that these people are already humans and citizens with the full rights that the officer him- or herself has, without resorting to an alienated and alienating investigation of documents, proof of origin, or the like, let alone a long process of 'acculturation' before universal rights could be assumed.

However, the current trends are mixed, and the global picture somewhat unclear. During the 1990s, global income inequality, polarisation, poverty, and social exclusion grew substantially. These maladies have a disproportionate impact on young people: four out of five people under the age of 20 are living in developing countries. Although, through their use of ICTs, young people are among the most active builders of the new world, there are obstacles in the way of their prefigurative role as ambassadors of the digital era. In addition to the material and structural barriers preventing their voices from being heard through the Internet and other ICTs, they are also held back by their cultural, social and economic position within the family and the surrounding society. Thus, if we claim that 'it is young people who take a lead in creative practices using digital media' (Erstad 2008, p. 185), we should acknowledge the existing and emerging digital inequities among young people and the obstacles to their participation in digital culture. These gaps cannot be bridged without taking into account the very principles of anonymous collectivism and radical inclusiveness that are central characteristics of the Wikiworld.

A lengthy debate about the sustainability of Western values has taken place in both public and academic arenas. Over the years, many thinkers have accepted that it is imperative fundamentally to rethink Western values. One such commentator, Stephen Toulmin (1998), a noted philosopher, has foreseen the gradual termination of the age of Enlightenment. He has suggested that the agenda of the Enlightenment could be experiencing a shift in emphasis from the written to the oral, from the universal to the particular, from the general to the local and from the timeless to the timely. Moreover, Toulmin has stressed that human beings need to learn that they can never rule or control the world entirely. Sociologists and philosophers share the view that unregulated economic globalisation is ultimately unable to guarantee welfare for all.

In a manifesto titled 'Autonomous Global University', the members of the Vidya Ashram collective recognise the colonialisation of knowledge in clear terms:

> [The] Twentieth century has been a century of knowledge production. It has also been a century of unprecedented violence. The knowledge that we produce is eventually turned against ourselves and against the whole society. While this was also true of the modern university, [the] knowledge society that is in the making now seems to be singularly designed to appropriate knowledge and turn it against the producers of knowledge in the service of global capital and global machineries of violence. (Vidya Ashram 2008)

However, given this analysis, the cure is also clearly defined. Local knowledges, *lokvidya* in Hindi, are the native skills and types of knowledge that have been repressed and belittled by rabid forms of Western enlightenment and corporate appropriation, but that have always supported the existence of multiple worldviews and lifestyles.

If we grant that there is no hierarchy among various locations of knowledge in society and that all kinds of knowledge have a role to play in the reconstruction of society, grounds for non-hierarchical solidarities across many boundaries are prepared. Moreover, the epistemic recognition of *lokvidya* opens us up to a vast realm of living knowledge traditions in society as forms of autonomous knowledge activity. This also creates the condition for people to see their own knowledge traditions as sources of strength, and not only as means of survival (ibid.).

Local forms of knowledge are antidotes to the agenda of the global power elite. If we don't embrace the idea of co-operation, the world could be the victim of destructive unilateralism, a situation in which one power structure could determine economic-technological development, military and knowledge production, deepening digital, economic and cultural divides, as well as human suffering, cultural conflicts and ecological catastrophes. This type of unilateralism would mean reinforcing the advantage of the North. There would be discussion on the elimination of obstacles to free trade, while the position of the better-off countries would no doubt remain secure, and new ICTs would be invented behind the digital divide. Furthermore, the North would use the South as a dumping ground for old ICTs. This course of action has a long and dishonourable history in the areas of foreign trade and so-called multilateral co-operation.

The other option would be multilateralism or internationalism where the guiding principle would be sustainable development and where high and low technologies would exist in tandem, appropriately adapted to local circumstances. However, the fundamental question about how ICTs and the digital divide relate to the process of global development is not about technology, nor is it about politics. Instead, it concerns global politics and local practices. In sociological literature, this dualistic perception has been termed glocalisation. In brief, glocalisation means that the world is experienced as one place: the global is an aspect of the local, and vice versa (Beck 1999, p. 101). Young people in particular have a tendency to develop a glocal consciousness. In the field of global politics, when seeking to establish a global economy, we should also aim at global democratic structures and global legislation. It seems likely that international laws and regulations as well as a profound shift in values are needed for people to grasp the ethical responsibility of the human being as *Homo proteus*, a species that in a fundamental way creates its own environments.

The UN committee overseeing the execution of the International Convention on Economic, Social and Cultural Rights proposes three objectives for poverty reduction (Robinson 2002). These comprise equal rights, participation and inclusion. In our opinion, these principles might also prove useful in the discussion on participatory digital democracy and ways of bridging the digital divide. However, these principles are only ideological starting points: their implementation in practice requires real local action. Building digital democracy through ICTs will achieve nothing unless administrative structures and channels of participation are also in place. As Malina (1999, p. 38) puts it, 'where normative aspects and genuine democratic practice are absent, and where citizens are held in low regard or excluded by their representatives and other experts in the public sphere, outcomes for democratic autonomy, more participatory democracy and social cohesion will be gloomy'.

Numerous local experiments making practical use of ICTs in various parts of the world offer some hope. It is characteristic of this activity that ICTs are made to function as part of local circumstances. The adoption of ICTs in itself is not important: instead, the technologies are harnessed to solve a practical problem, be it the transmission of information (distribution of weather- or health-related information) or the provision of a technical solution (for example, water pumps operating on solar energy). The second important characteristic of this type of development activity is the utilisation of local knowledge that may not exist in written form but constitutes orally transmitted information manifesting itself in local customs and activities. It is typical of these experiments that new innovations are created through combining new technologies with existing techniques that may have been in use for a long time. Furthermore, it is crucial to grasp the importance of focusing on the use and development of technology that responds to people's actual needs – a principle that is a welcome guideline for sustainable development in the field of information and communication technologies in general. As researchers, it is crucial to emerge from our ivory towers and fancy laboratories and act as anthropologists, collecting data in the field and creating solutions in close co-operation with locals. All in all, experiments like these realise positive and reformative values such as sharing, listening and socio-diversity.

Amartya Sen (2002, p. 51), a Nobel Prize-winning economist, has promoted the idea of sharing to help overcome the global maladies of the contemporary economic world order. Perceiving sharing as one of the central notions in the general culture of science, Sen argues that the organising principles of sharing might have something valuable and substantial to offer in the seemingly endless battle against pervasive poverty, deprivation, and the ongoing conflicts that result from global confrontations between the economic elite and those who have nothing to lose but their chains. The market mechanism functions as an organisational ideology, which leads to unpredictable and often unsatisfactory social consequences. Sen contrasts the idea of sharing to the use of the market mechanism as a dominant ideology in the current era. For Sen, economic development is about neither the accumulation of capital nor the growth of gross national product but the means of expanding human freedom through sharing the common good.

In the end, there are two opposing arguments concerning the overall meaning of ICTs. The first, proposed by ICT enthusiasts, claims that, as vehicles for the economy and knowledge production, new technologies will improve everyone's standard of living. For this reason, everyone should have access to information, and it is not necessary to wait for more basic needs to be met before moving on to the Internet age. The second argument, from ICT critics, stresses the importance of meeting basic needs such as democratic governance, food resources, health care, social security and education before attending to problems such as the digital divide. Both arguments are valid if we recognise that ICTs are not natural resources but human-made objects that can be used in a variety of ways. ICTs are technologies, but not only technologies. For we as people always maintain some kind of relationship to these technologies. We can use the ICT imperative as an excuse for our own thoughtlessness and apparent inability to make reasonable decisions. However, if we consider the matter logically, we will see that ICTs have no power over us. In this basic sense, ICTs may be good servants, but they are certainly bad masters. The emphasis should then be on how to use them, and to what end. One answer lies in the development and use of socialist media as discussed in the previous chapter.

In furthering socialist media and its allied social inventions such as welfare structures, including basic income, it is vitally important to note that there is more wealth and prosperity in the world today than at any point in history, and yet economic, social and technological divisions run deeper than ever. In this situation, it is important to focus on the ways which ICTs might be applied in different parts of the world. ICTs cannot be thought of as simply a technology: they are loaded with cultural values and preferences, as well as desires for what tomorrow should look like. It is clear that those values are largely Western, with a particular emphasis on North America and its allies in consumer capitalism.

Many Western values such as individual freedom of speech and equal opportunities are easy to subscribe to in theory but quite hard to actualise in reality. From the view point of ICTs, these values also contain a number of less commendable ideas, such as the notion of commercial profit as the most important outcome of the proliferation of ICTs. Yet, it is this particular outcome that is given priority in an ICT industry dominated by a handful of media giants. It is in the interest of these corporations to act as the ambassadors of goodwill until it is time to calculate profitability. The supply of goodwill lasts only as long as the investment is expected to generate profit. Thus it is important to realise that someone like Bill Gates is an opportunist who seized the moment by using the capitalist system for his own individual purposes. The question is not why do we tolerate Gates's business – his goal 'to make capitalism more creative' – but how is the capitalist system structured? What is wrong with it, that an individual can achieve such disproportionate power (Žižek 2007b, p. 235)? This very same question regarding the perverse logic of capitalism should also be asked with regard to the operations of various official bodies such as the UN, UNICEF (United Nations Children's Fund) and NGOs advocating co-operation between the private sector, the public sector and civil society. In the final analysis, whose interests are served?

Moreover, the possibility of bridging the ICT gap and making a profit is in many cases completely out of the question; especially in sparsely populated areas, profit is hard to make. At this point, we come down to a question of values: What kind of world do we want our children to inherit? Today, young people under 20 years of age make up a fifth of the world's population, some 1.2 billion people. The importance of investing in their lives cannot be overestimated, as the knowledge, skills and attitudes learned in youth often determine a person's future. It is our view that a world where young people, remaining in their own localities, can generate their own culture and connect with youth in other parts of the globe to exchange ideas and learn from each other would be a global village worth living in.

As Alexander Bard and Jan Söderqvist (2002, pp. xi–xii) remind us: 'The WTC hijackers were very well educated and very much at home on the Net. These guys even booked their plane tickets online. They possessed the necessary financial means, but more importantly, the necessary networking skills, to make their plans work.' But this is not the end of the story. We, too, as Westerners, must reflect on our uses and misuses of education. For it can be argued that in the last decades of neo-liberal rubbish we have failed in our educational policies to pose the most fundamental questions concerning the overall good of society and the world. We can even say that, due to self-reinforcing processes of economic growth, population growth, technological expansion, arms races, and growing income inequality, humanity is in a state of crisis that cannot be solved with any conceivable quick fixes like leaning on the promises of ICTs. It is shocking to realise – and this realisation should shake us up as academics and teachers at the tertiary level – that people with higher degrees do the greatest harm when it comes to the problems we have described. 'This realisation arises from the observation that the vast majority of people in crucial decision-making positions have tertiary qualifications' (Lautensach and Lautensach 2009). And it is they who make the most ill-advised, short-sighted and self-serving decisions: 'An empirical correlation appears evident between higher education and inadequate decision-making' (ibid.).

In conclusion, we would like to suggest that in future, instead of ceding power to a seemingly ignorant elite, the people – educators, students, activists, parents – should take the initiative – as is already happening in various localities around the globe. Real advances in the area of digital literacy can be made only if the power to learn is grasped by educative communities that contribute locally and connect globally. People are already working together outside of the formal schooling system, official state bureaucracy, the authoritarian state, and so on. No one knows what the consequences of this turn away from public policy and from the state itself will be, and that, of course, can be frightening. It may be that all previous truths and certainties are more or less lost, but as John Holloway (2005, p. 215) reminds us, 'the openness of uncertainty is central to revolution'. Perhaps also for the state's institutional players this 'openness of uncertainty' is their only chance of acting productively and doing their democratic duty. Otherwise they have no role in the digital revolution. By ceding their centralised power to define problems and solutions to the communities of digital practitioners they could make a strong case for furthering not only peoples' digital literacies and technological competencies, but also their self-regulated socio-political trans-formation. For, as Giroux (2004, p. 84) aptly puts it:

> one imperative of a critical pedagogy is to offer students opportunities to become aware of their potential and responsibility as individual and social agents to expand, struggle over, and deepen democratic values, institutions, and identities. They must help students unlearn the presupposition that

knowledge is unrelated to action, conception to implementation, and learning to social change. Knowledge in this case is more than understanding; it is also about the possibilities of self-determination, individual autonomy, and social agency.

And there is even more at stake, as Rudolf Bahro, an eco-socialist philosopher and educational reformist from the now defunct German Democratic Republic, had already noted in the late 1970s:

The production of surplus consciousness that is already in train spontaneously must be vigorously pursued in an active way, so as to produce quite intentionally a surplus of education which is so great, both quantitatively and qualitatively, that it cannot possibly be trapped in the existing structures of work and leisure time, so that the contradictions of these structures come to a head and their revolutionary transformation becomes indispensable. (1978, p. 404, quoted in Gorz 1997, p. 89)

The idea of the production of surplus consciousness takes us from formal freedom of education, however critical, to the realm of actual freedom, that of *educational superabundance*. This is the true goal of the Wikiworld. In our usage, the notion of educational superabundance refers to learning and being that is, strictly speaking, superfluous compared to the usual utilitarian education as appropriated in capitalist life; it is something more than is commonly tolerated in school or corporate bureaucracy. Educational abundance creates passionate and responsible collaboration among teachers, students, colleagues, and other fellow human beings. It is a means for revolutionary ends: once people can easily learn *more* than what is needed in working life, or in alienated consumerist everyday life, then wage slavery can be reduced to an absolute minimum and an autonomous world of convivial life is made possible.

We advocate, along with many others like Illich, Gorz and Bahro, the proliferation of native skills and forms of knowledge over and above the alienating skills and conditions of proletarian and precarious work. This is a revolutionary tendency with which we can wholeheartedly agree. But at the same time we must emphasise that educational superabundance is not only a means but also an end in itself. Education, modes of learning, forms of knowledge; the whole human heritage should not be treated as a tool, one of the 'resources' to be utilised in a world of 'means without ends'. Rather, we should see learning skills and acquiring knowledge in the light of perennial philosophy as ways for people to challenge and transform themselves together with others. Paraphrasing Žižek, educational revolution, as political revolution in the larger society, is made by living as if the revolution had already happened, as if the future was already here. This is where the germs of socialist media and promises of the Wikiworld enter the discussion. Modes of learning in the Wikiworld are not only a manifestation of radical openness of democracy and education, but also show in practice what emancipated people can do, what those who have decided to think for themselves can achieve in co-operation with others. It is already possible today to collaborate, use and distribute educational content without relying on corporations, governments, the market model university and other closed institutions. The open and superabundant world of education is here, if we want it.

REFERENCES

Aittola, Tapio, Riitta Koikkalainen and Esa Sironen (eds) (1995). *'Confronting Strangeness': Towards a Reflexive Modernization of the School*. Jyväskylä: Jyväskylän yliopisto.

Allman, Paula (1988). 'Gramsci, Freire and Illich: Their Contributions to Education for Socialism', in Tom Lovett (ed.), *Radical Approaches to Adult Education: A Reader*. London and New York: Routledge, pp. 85–113.

Annan, Kofi (2002a). 'Köyhille on annettava esimerkki talouden hyödyistä' [Poor People Need an Example of the Benefits of the Economy], *Helsingin Sanomat*, 8 February.

Annan, Kofi (2002b). 'Meksikon kokous ratkaisee miljoonien köyhien kohtalon' [Mexico Summit Decides the Fate of Millions of Poor People], *Helsingin Sanomat*, 21 March.

Antikainen, Aari, et al. (1996). *Living in a Learning Society*. London: Falmer Press.

Arendt, Hannah (1961). *Between Past and Future*. New York: Penguin Books.

Aronowitz, Stanley (2004). 'Against Schooling: Education and Social Class', *Workplace* 6 (1), http://www.louisville.edu/journal/workplace/issue6p1/aronowitz04.html (retrieved 26 February 2004).

Bahro, Rudolf (1978). *The Alternative in Eastern Europe*. London: New Left Books.

Bard, Alexander, and Jan Söderqvist Jan (2002). *Netocracy. New Power Elite and Life After Capitalism*. London: Pearson Education.

Baudrillard, Jean (1995). *Lopun illuusio eli tapahtumien lakko* [The End of Illusion, or the Strike of Events]. Trans. M. Määttänen. Helsinki: Gaudeamus.

Bauman, Zygmunt (1995). *Life in Fragments*. Cambridge: Blackwell.

Bauman, Zygmunt (1998). *Globalization. The Human Consequences*. Cambridge: Polity Press.

Bauwens, Michel (2005). 'The Political Economy of Peer Production', http://www.ctheory.net/articles.aspx?id=499 (retrieved 21 October 2007).

Beck, Ulrich (1995). 'Politiikan uudelleen keksiminen' [Reinventing Politics], in U. Beck, A. Giddens and S. Lash, *Nykyajan jäljillä* [In the Footsteps of Modernity]. Tampere: Vastapaino, pp. 11–82.

Beck, Ulrich (1999). *Mitä globalisaatio on?* [What is Globalisation?] Tampere: Vastapaino.

Beck, Ulrich (2002). 'The Cosmopolitan Society and Its Enemies', *Theory, Culture & Society* 19 (1–2): 17–44.

Beckedahl, Marcus (2006) 'John Perry Barlow on Civil Disobedience in a Digital World', interview with John Perry Barlow on the 23rd Chaos Communication Congress (23C3) Berlin, 29 December 2006, http://www.netzpolitik.org/2007/netzpolitiktv-john-perry-barlow-ueber-zivilen-ungehorsam/ (retrieved 28 February 2007).

Beigbeder, Frédéric (2004). *24.99.* Helsinki: Like.

Bhana, Surenda (1975). The Tolstoy Farm: Gandhi's Experiment in 'Cooperative Commonwealth'. *South African Historical Journal* 7, http://www.anc.org.za/ancdocs/history/people/gandhi/bhana.html.

Bok, Derek (2003). *Universities in the Marketplace.* Princeton: Princeton University Press.

Borradori, Giovanna (ed.) (2003). *Philosophy in a Time of Terror: Dialogues with Jürgen Habermas and Jacques Derrida.* Chicago: Chicago University Press.

Brookfield, Stephen (1995). *Becoming a Critically Reflective Teacher.* San Francisco: Jossey-Bass.

Bruffee, Kenneth (1981). 'Collaborative Learning', *College English* 43 (7): 745–7.

Bruffee, Kenneth (1995). 'Sharing Our Toys', *Change* 27 (1): 12–19.

Bruner, Jerome (1996). *Culture of Education.* Cambridge, MA: Harvard University Press.

Buckingham, David (2000). *After the Death of Childhood. Growing Up in the Age of Electronic Media.* Cambridge: Polity Press.

Burawoy, Michael (2006). 'A Public Sociology for Human Rights', in J. Blau and K. Iyall-Smith (eds), *Public Sociologies Reader.* Boulder: Rowman & Littlefield, http://burawoy.berkeley.edu/PS/Public%20Sociology%20for%20Human%20Rights.pdf/ (retrieved 18 September 2009).

Burbules, Nicholas, and Carlos Torres (eds) (2000). *Globalization and Education: Critical Perspectives.* New York and London: Routledge.

Cape Town Open Education Declaration. http://www.capetowndeclaration.org/read-the-declaration (retrieved 21 February 2008).

Carlson, Chris (2007). 'Venezuela Launches Sale of "Bolivarian" Computers', Venezuelanalysis.com, http://www.venezuelanalysis.com/news/2441 (retrieved 8 December 2007).

Castells, Manuel (1996). *The Rise of the Network Society.* Oxford: Blackwell.

Castells, Manuel (2000). 'Informationalismi ja verkostoyhteiskunta' [Informationalism and Newtork Society], epilogue in P. Himanen,

Hakkerietiikka ja informaatioajan henki [Hacker Ethics and the Spirit of the Information Age]. Helsinki: WSOY. See also http://annenberg.usc.edu/Faculty/Communication/~/media/Faculty/Facpdfs/Informationalism%20pdf.ashx (retrieved 6 September 2009).

Castells, Manuel (2001). *The Internet Galaxy. Reflections on the Internet, Business, and Society*. Oxford: Oxford University Press.

CBS News (2003) 'Al-Jazeera Site Clicks with Net Users', 2 April.

Chomsky, Noam (2000). *Chomsky on MisEducation*. Ed. Donaldo Macedo. Lanham: Rowman & Littlefield.

Chomsky, Noam (2001). *9-11*. New York: Open Media.

Coles, P. (2002). 'Barefoot Pioneers', *New Scientist* 174 (2341): 40–3.

Cross, Tom (2006). 'Puppy Smoothies: Improving the Reliability of Open, Collaborative Wikis', *First Monday* 11 (9), http://www.firstmonday.org/issues/issue11_9/cross/index.html (retrieved 18 September 2006).

Darder, Antonio, Rodolfo Torres and Marta Baltodano (eds) (2003). *The Critical Pedagogy Reader*. London and New York: Routledge.

Deleuze, Gilles, and Felix Guattari (1987). *A Thousand Plateaus: Capitalism and Schizophrenia*. Minnesota: University of Minnesota Press.

Deleuze, Gilles, and Felix Guattari (1993). *Mitä filosofia on?* [What is Philosophy?] Helsinki: Gaudeamus.

Derrida, Jacques (2002). *Negotiations. Interventions and Interviews*. Ed., trans., and with an introduction by Elizabeth Rottenberg. Stanford: Stanford University Press.

Drahos, Peter, and John Braithwaite (2002). *Information Feudalism. Who Owns the Knowledge Economy?* London: Earthscan.

Dreyfus, Hubert (2001). *On the Internet*. London: Routledge.

Dwight, Jim, and Jim Garrison (2003). 'A Manifesto for Instructional Technology: Hyperpedagogy', *Teachers College Record* 105 (5): 699–728.

Engeström, Y., and D. Middleton (eds) (1996) *Cognition and Communication at Work*. Cambridge: Cambridge University Press.

Erstad, Ole (2008). 'Trajectories of Remixing. Digital Literacies, Media Production, and Schooling', in Colin Lankshear and Michele Knobel (eds), *Digital Literacies*. New York: Peter Lang, pp. 177–202.

Eskola, Antti (1968). *Suomi sulo Pohjola* [Finland, Charming North]. Helsinki: Kirjayhtymä.

Evans, Mary (2004). *Killing Thinking. The Death of the Universities*. New York: Continuum.

Feenberg, Andrew (1998). 'Can Technology Incorporate Values? Marcuse's Answer to the Question of the Age', http://dogma.free.fr/txt/AF_MarcuseTechnology.htm (retrieved 21 October 2006).

Fornäs, Johan (1995). *Cultural Theory and Late Modernity*. London: Sage.

Foucault, Michel (1979). *Discipline and Punish*. New York: Vintage Books.

Foucault, Michel (1988). 'The Masked Philosopher', in *Politics, Philosophy, Culture*. Ed. Lawrence D. Kritzman. New York: Routledge.

Foucault, Michel (1994). *The Order of Things*. New York: Vintage Books.

Freire, Paulo (2005). *Pedagogy of the Oppressed* (30th Anniversary Edition). New York: Continuum. (Originally published 1970). Also http://www.marxists.org/subject/education/freire/pedagogy (retrieved 24 July 2006).

Fromm, Erich (1963). 'The Revolutionary Character', in *The Dogma of Christ and Other Essays on Religion, Psychology, and Culture*. New York: Holt, Rinehart & Winston, http://www.angelfire.com/or/sociologyshop/rchar.html.

Fromm, Erich (1970). *The Revolution of Hope*. New York: Harper & Row Publishers.

Fromm, Erich (1971). Introduction to Ivan Illich's *Celebration of Awareness*. London: Calder & Boyas. Also http://www.cogsci.ed.ac.uk/~ira/illich/texts (retrieved 10 March 2008).

Fromm, Erich (1996). *To Have or to Be?* New York: Continuum.

Galeano, Eduardo (2001). *Upside Down. A Primer for the Looking-Glass World*. Trans. Mark Fried. New York: Picador.

Galtung, Johan (2003). *The Role of the Intellectual II – This Time as Other-Criticism*, http://www.transcend.org./tpu (retrieved 26 December 2003).

Giles, Jim (2005). 'Internet Encyclopaedias Go Head to Head', http://www.nature.com/nature/journal/v438/n7070/full/438900a.html (retrieved 23 July 2006).

Giroux, Henry (1992). *Border Crossings*. New York and London: Routledge.

Giroux, Henry (1994). *Disturbing Pleasures*. New York: Routledge.

Giroux, Henry (1995) 'Pulp Fiction and the Cultural Studies', *Harvard Educational Review* 65 (2): 299–314.

Giroux, Henry (1996). *Fugitive Cultures*. New York and London: Routledge.

Giroux, Henry (2000a). *Impure Acts. The Practical Politics of Cultural Studies*. New York and London: Routledge.

Giroux, Henry (2000b). 'Representations of Violence, Popular Culture, and Demonization of Youth', in Stephanie Spina (ed.), *Smoke and Mirrors*. Lanham: Rowman & Littlefield, pp. 93–105.

Giroux, Henry (2001). *Public Places, Private Lives. Beyond the Culture of Cynicism*. Lanham: Rowman & Littlefield.

Giroux, Henry (2003a). 'Dystopian Nightmares and Educated Hopes: The Return of the Pedagogical and the Promise of Democracy', *Policy Futures in Education* 1 (3): 467–87, http://dx.doi.org/10.2304/pfie.2003.1.3.3 (retrieved 10 March 2008).

Giroux, Henry (2003b). 'Selling Out Higher Educatio', *Policy Futures in Education* 1 (1): 179–200, http://www.wwwords.co.uk/pfie/content/pdfs/1/issue1_1.asp#9 (retrieved 25 July 2006).

Giroux, Henry (2004). 'Academic Culture, Intellectual Courage, and the Crisis of Politics in an Era of Permanent War', in Henry Giroux and Susan Searls Giroux, *Take Back Higher Education*. New York: Palgrave Macmillan.

Giroux, Henry (2006). *Beyond the Spectacle of Terrorism: Global Uncertainty and the Challenge of the New Media*. Boulder: Paradigm Publishers.

Giroux, Henry, and Susan Searls Giroux (2004). 'Neoliberalism Goes to College: Higher Education in the New Economy', in Henry Giroux and Susan Searls Giroux, *Take Back Higher Education*. New York: Palgrave Macmillan.

González-Barahona, Jesus M., M. A. Ortuño Pérez, P. de las Heras Quirós, J. Centeno González and V. Matellán Olivera (2002). 'Counting Potatoes: The Size of Debian 2.2', http://people.debian.org/~jgb/debian-counting/counting-potatoes/ (retrieved 4 October 2006).

Gorz, André (1997). *Farewell to the Working Class*. London: Pluto Press.

Gorz, André (1999). *Reclaiming Work. Beyond the Wage-Based Society*. Cambridge: Polity Press.

Gramsci, Antonio (1971). *Selections from the Prison Notebooks of Antonio Gramsci*. Trans. Q. Hoare and G. Novell-Smith. New York: International Publishers.

Habermas, Jürgen (1981). *Theorie des kommunikativen Handelns*. Frankfurt am Main: Suhrkamp.

Habermas, Jürgen (1989). *The Theory of Communicative Action*, Vol. 2. Trans. T. McCarthy. Boston: Beacon Press.

Hamilton, Mary (2005). 'Sustainable Literacies and the Ecology of Lifelong Learning'. Working Papers of the Global Colloquium on Supporting Lifelong Learning online, Milton Keynes: Open University, http://www.open.ac.uk/lifelong-learning/papers/index.html (retrieved 7 October 2006).

Hand, Michael, and Barry Sandywell (2002). 'E-topia as Cosmopolis or Citadel. On the Democratizing and De-democratizing Logics of the Internet, or, Toward a Critique of the New Technological Fetishism', *Theory, Culture & Society* 19 (1–2): 197–225.

Hardt, Michael, and Antonio Negri (2000). *Empire*. Cambridge, MA, and London: Harvard University Press.

Hardt, Michael, and Antonio Negri (2004). *Multitude*. London: The Penguin Press.

Heidegger, Martin (1962). *Being and Time*. London: SCM Press.

Heidegger, Martin (1982). *The Question Concerning Technology*. Harper Perennial.

Hewlett, Nick (2007). *Badiou, Balibar, Rancière: Rethinking Emancipation*. London: Continuum.

Himanen, Pekka (2000). *Hakkerietiikka ja informaatioajan henki* [Hacker Ethics and the Spirit of the Information Age]. Helsinki: WSOY.

Holloway, John (2005). *Change the World Without Taking Power. The Meaning of Revolution Today*. London: Pluto Press.

Holst, John (2002). *Social Movements, Civil Society, and Radical Adult Education*. Westport and London: Bergin & Garvey.

Honderich, Ted (2003). *After the Terror*. Edinburgh: Edinburgh University Press.

Huff, Toby (2006). 'The Big Shift', *Society* 43 (4): 30–4.

Illich, Ivan (1971). *Deschooling Society*. New York: Harper & Row Publishers. Also http://reactor-core.org/deschooling.html.

Illich, Ivan (1980). *Tools for Conviviality*. New York: Harper & Row, http://opencollector.org/history/homebrew/tools.html (retrieved 15 October 2006).

Illich, Ivan (1996) Foreword in M. Hern (ed.), *Deschooling Our Lives*. Philadelphia: New Society Publishers.

Jenkins, Henry (1998). 'Introduction: Childhood Innocence and Other Modern Myths', in H. Jenkins (ed.), *The Children's Culture Reader*. New York and London: New York University Press, pp. 1–37.

Jenkins, Henry, with Katie Clinton, Ravi Purushotma, Alice J. Robison and Margaret Weigel (2006). 'Confronting the Challenges of Participatory Culture: Media Education for the 21st Century'. MacArthur Foundation, http://www.macfound.org/site/apps/n1net/ (retrieved 15 October 2006).

Kahn, Richard, and Douglas Kellner (2006). 'Reconstructing Technoliteracy: A Multiple Literacies Approach', http://www.gseis.ucla.edu/faculty/kellner/index.html (retrieved 12 December 2006).

Kalathil, Shanthi, and Taylor C. Boas (2003), 'The Conventional Wisdom: What Lies Beneath?', in *Open Networks, Closed Regimes: The Impact of the Internet on Authoritarian Rule*, Carnegie Endowment for International Peace; *First Monday* 8 (1), http://www.firstmonday.dk/issues/issue8_1/kalathil/kalathil_chapter1.html (retrieved 2 April 2004).

Kant, Immanual (1784). 'An Answer to the Question: What is Enlightenment', http://www.english.upenn.edu/~mgamer/Etexts/kant.html (retrieved 13 October 2006).

Katz, John (1997). *Virtuous Reality*. New York: Random House.

Kauppi, Piia-Noora, and Alexander Stubb (2004). 'Suomen on herättävä terrorin todellisuuteen' [Finland Must Wake Up to the Reality of Terror], *Aamulehti* 24 (3): A2.

Kellner, Douglas (1995). *Media Culture. Cultural Studies, Identity and Politics Between the Modern and the Postmodern*. New York and London: Routledge.

Kellner, Douglas (1998a). 'Multiple Literacies and Critical Pedagogy in a Multicultural Society', *Educational Theory* 48 (1): 102–22.

Kellner, Douglas (1998b). 'From 1984 to One-Dimensional Man: Critical Reflections on Orwell and Marcuse', http://www.uta.edu/huma/illuminations/kell13.htm (retrieved 21 October 2006).

Kellner, Douglas (2000). 'Globalization and New Social Movements: Lessons for Critical Theory and Pedagogy', in Nicholas Burbules and Carlos Alberto Torres (eds), *Globalization and Education: Critical Perspectives*. New York and London: Routledge, pp. 299–321.

Kellner, Douglas (2004). 'Technological Transformation, Multiple Literacies, and the Re-visioning of Education', *E-Learning* (1) 1, http://www.wwwords.co.uk/elea/content/pdfs/1/issue1_1.asp#2 (retrieved 21 October 2006).

Kellner, Douglas, and Richard Kahn (2006). 'Reconstructing Techno-literacy: A Multiple Literacies Approach', http://www.gseis.ucla.edu/faculty/kellner/index.html (retrieved 6 October 2006).

Kincheloe, Joe (2007). 'Critical Pedagogy in the Twenty-first Century', in Peter McLaren and Joe Kincheloe (eds), *Critical Pedagogy. Where Are We Now?* New York: Peter Lang, pp. 9-42.

Kinder, Marsha (ed.) (1999) *Kids' Media Culture*. Durham and London: Duke University Press.

Klein, Naomi (2000). *No Logo*. London: Flamingo.

Klein, Naomi (2002). *Fences and Windows: Dispatches from the Frontlines of the Globalization Debate*. London: Flamingo.

Kvale, Steinar (1997) 'Research Apprenticeship', *Nordisk pedagogik* 17 (3): 186–94.

Kvale, Steinar, and K. Nielsen (1997) 'Current Issues of Apprenticeship', *Nordisk pedagogik* 17 (3): 130–9.

La Page, M. (2002). 'Village-Life.Com', *New Scientist* 174 (2341): 44–5.

Lankshear, Colin, and Michele Knobel (2003). *New Literacies. Changing Knowledge and Classroom Learning*. Buckingham: Open University Press.

Lankshear, Colin, and Michele Knobel (2005). 'Digital Literacies: Policy, Pedagogy and Research Considerations for Education', http://www.geocities.com/c.lankshear/Oslo.pdf (retrieved 26 March 2006).

Lankshear, Colin, and Michele Knobel (2006). 'Blogging as Participation: The Active Sociality of a New Literacy', http://www.geocities.com/c.lankshear/bloggingparticipation.pdf (retrieved 27 April 2006).

Lankshear, Colin, and Michele Knobel (2008). 'Introduction. Digital Literacies – Concepts, Policies and Practices', in Colin Lankshear and Michele Knobel (eds), *Digital Literacies*. New York: Peter Lang, pp. 1–32.

Lankshear, Colin, Michael Peters and Michele Knobel (1996). 'Critical Pedagogy and Cyberspace', in H. Teoksessa Giroux, C. Lankshear, P. McLaren and M. Peters (eds), *Counternarratives. Cultural Studies and Critical Pedagogies in Postmodern Space*. New York and London: Routledge, pp. 149–88.

Lash, Scott (2002). *Critique of Information*. London: Sage.

Lautensach, Alexander, and Sabina Lautensach (2009). 'A Curriculum for a Secure Future: Agenda for Reform', in Juha Suoranta, Donna Houston, Gregory Martin and Peter McLaren (eds), *Havoc of Capitalism. Educating for Social and Environmental Justice*. Amsterdam: Sense Publishers.

Lave, Jane, and Etienne Wenger (1991). *Situated Learning*. Cambridge: Cambridge University Press.

Leinonen, Teemu, Tere Vadén and Juha Suoranta (2007). 'Wikiversity for Free Education and Free School: a New Initiative for Global Capacity Building?', http://en.wikiversity.org/wiki/Wikiversity:Free_education_and_free_school%3F (retrieved 5 August 2009).

Lenin, V. I. (1916). 'Imperialism, the Highest Stage of Capitalism', http://www.marxists.org/archive/lenin/works/1916/imp-hsc/ch05.htm (retrieved 7 October 2006).

Lessig, Lawrence (2001). *The Future of Ideas. The Fate of the Commons in a Connected World*. New York: Random House.

Lessig, Lawrence (2006). 'On the Economies of Culture', http://www.lessig.org/blog/2006/09/on_the_economies_of_culture.html (retrieved 6 September 2009).

Lie, Truls, and Jacques Rancière (2006). 'Our Police Order: What Can Be Said, Seen, and Done', http://www.eurozine.com/articles/2006-08-11-lieranciere-en.html (retrieved 12 December 2007).

Light, Jennifer (2001). 'Rethinking the Digital Divide', *Harvard Educational Review* 71 (4): 709–33.

Lyotard, Jean-François (1984). *The Postmodern Condition: A Report on Knowledge*. Minneapolis: University of Minnesota Press. Also http://www.marxists.org/reference/subject/philosophy/works/fr/lyotard.htm (retrieved 24 July 2006).

Macalister, Terry (2006). 'Soviet Power Falls to City of London with Series of Energy Flotations', http://business.guardian.co.uk./story/0..1830940.00.html (retrieved 7 October 2006).

Macrine, Sheila (2009). *Critical Pedagogy in Uncertain Times: Hopes and Possibilities*. New York: Palgrave Macmillan.

Malina, Anna (1999). 'Perspectives on Citizen Democratisation and Alienation in the Virtual Public Sphere', in B. Hague and B. Loader (eds), *Digital Democracy. Discourse and Decision Making in the Information Age*. London and New York: Routledge, pp. 23–38.

Malnuit, Olivier (2006). 'Pourquoi les gèants du business se prennent-ils pour Jésus?' [Why are the Giants of Business Turning to Jesus?], *Technikart* (February): 32–7.

Marcuse, Herbert (1941). 'Some Social Implications of Modern Technology', *Studies in Philosophy and Social Science* 9 (3): 414–39.

Marx, Karl (1844). 'The Economic and Philosophical Manuscripts', http://www.marxists.org/archive/marx/works/1844/epm/ (retrieved 6 September 2009).

Marx, Karl (1858). 'The Grundrisse. Outlines of the Critique of Political Economy', http://www.marxists.org/archive/marx/works/1857/grundrisse/ch14.htm (retrieved 4 October 2006).

Marx, Karl (1859). 'A Contribution to the Critique of Political Economy', http://www.marxists.org/archive/marx/works/1859/critique-pol-economy/preface-abs.htm (retrieved 23 March 2007).

Marx, Karl (1867). '*Capital*, Vol. One', http://www.marxists.org/archive/marx/works/1867-c1/ch33.htm (retrieved 13 February 2007).

Marx, Karl (1875). 'Critique of the Gotha Program', http://www.marxists.org/archive/marx/works/1875/gotha/ch01.htm (retrieved 21 October 2006).

May, Christopher (2001). *The Information Society. The Sceptical View*. Cambridge: Polity Press.

McChesney, Robert (1998). 'The Political Economy of Global Communication', in R. W. McChesney, et al. (eds), *Capitalism and the Information Age. The Political Economy of the Global Communication Revolution*. New York: Monthly Review Press.

McChesney, Robert (1999). *Rich Media, Poor Democracy*. New York: The New Press.

McChesney, Robert, and John Nichols (2002). *Our Media, Not Theirs. The Democratic Struggle Against Corporate Media*. New York: Seven Stories Press.

McLaren, Peter (1995). *Critical Pedagogy and Predatory Culture*. New York and London: Routledge.

McLaren, Peter (1997). *Revolutionary Multiculturalism. Pedagogies of Dissent for the New Millenium*. Boulder: Westview Press.

McLaren, Peter (2000). *Che Guevara, Paulo Freire, and the Pedagogy of Revolution*. Lanham: Rowman & Littlefield.

McLaren, Peter, and Nathalia Jaramillo (2007). *Pedagogy and Praxis in the Age of Empire – Towards a New Humanism*. Rotterdam: Sense Publishers.

McLaren, Peter, and Joe Kincheloe (eds), *Critical Pedagogy. Where Are We Now?* New York: Peter Lang.

Mead, Margaret (1971). *Ikäryhmien ristiriidat. Sukupolvikuilun tutkimusta* [Culture and Commitment. A Study of the Generation Gap]. Helsinki: Otava.

Merten, Stefan (2000). 'GNU/Linux – Milestone on the Way to the GPL Society', http://www.opentheory.org/gplsociety/text.phtml (retrieved 4 October 2006).

Mikkonen, Teemu, Tere Vadén and Niklas Vainio (2007). 'The Protestant Ethic Strikes Back: Open Source Developers and the Ethic of Capitalism', *First Monday* 12 (2) (February), http://www.firstmonday.org/issues/issue12_2/mikkonen/index.html.

Morss, John (2003). '"Looking Allies": Gilles Deleuze as Critical Theorist', in Michael Peters, Mark Olssen and Colin Lankshear (eds), *Futures of Critical Theory. Dreams of Difference*. Lanham: Rowman & Littlefield, pp. 127–39.

Nietzsche, Friedrich (1996) *Human, All Too Human*. Cambridge: Cambridge University Press.

Noble, David (2003). *Digital Diploma Mills*. New York: Monthy Review Press.

Norris, Pippa (2001). *Digital Divide. Civic Engagement, Information Poverty, and the Internet Worldwide*. Cambridge: Cambridge University Press.

Nowotny, Helga (2000). 'Transgressive Competence: The Narrative of Expertise', *European Journal of Social Theory* 3 (1): 5–21.

O'Hara, Kieron, and David Stevens (2006). *Inequality.com. Power, Poverty and the Digital Divide*. Oxford: Oneworld.

Papert, Seymort (1996). *The Connected Family. Bridging the Digital Generation Gap*. Atlanta: Longstreet.

Parker, Ian (2007). *Revolution in Psychology. Alienation to Emancipation*. London: Pluto Press.

Peshkin, Alan (1994) *Growing Up American*. Prospect Heights: Waveland Press.

'Pessi' (2004). *Kyllästyttääkö?* [Bored?]. *Aamulehti, Allakka* (3–11 April): 40.

Peters, Michael (2004). Editorial, 'Marxist Futures: Knowledge Socialism and the Academy', *Policy Futures in Education* 2 (3 and 4), http://www.wwwords.co.uk/pfie/content/pdfs/2/issue2_3.asp#1 (retrieved 12 October 2006).

Peters, Michael, and Colin Lankshear (1996). 'Critical Literacy and Critical Texts', *Educational Theory* 46 (1): 51–70.

Pfaller, Robert (2000). *Interpassivität: Studien über delegiertes Genießen* [Interpassivity: Study on Delegated Enjoyment]. Berlin: Springer.

Postman, Neil (1996). *The End of Education*. New York: Vintage Books.

Postman, Neil, and Charles Weingartner (1971). *Teaching As Subversive Activity*. New York: Delta.

Putnam, Robert (2000). *Bowling Alone. The Collapse and Revival of American Community*. New York: Simon & Schuster.

Rancière, Jacques (1988). 'Good Times or Pleasure at the Barriers', in John Moore, Adrian Rifkin and Roger Thomas (eds), *Voices of the People. The Social Life of 'La Sociale' at the End of the Second Empire*. London and New York: Routledge & Kegan Paul, pp. 45–94.

Rancière, Jacques (1991). *The Ignorant Schoolmaster*. Stanford: Stanford University Press.

Rantala, Leena, and Juha Suoranta (2008). 'Digital Literacy Policies in the EU – Inclusive Partnership as the Final Stage of Governmentality?', in Colin Lankshear and Michele Knobel (eds), *Digital Literacies*. New York: Peter Lang.

Rawls, John (1971). *A Theory of Justice*. Cambridge, MA: Harvard University Press.

Robins, Kevin, and Frank Webster (1999). *Times of the Technoculture: From the Information Society to Virtual Life*. New York and London: Routledge.

Robinson, Mary (2002). Äärimmäinen köyhyys on pahin ihmisoikeu- songelma [Extreme Poverty is the Worst Human Rights Problem]. *Helsingin Sanomat*, 19 April.

Roy, Arundhati (2004). 'Do Turkeys Enjoy Thanksgiving? A Global Resistance to Empire', http://zmag.org/content/showarticle.cfm?Secti onID=15&ItemID=4873 (retrieved 13 February 2004).

Rushkoff, Douglas (1996). *Playing the Future. How Kids' Culture Can Teach Us to Thrive in an Age of Chaos*. New York: HarperCollins.

Rushkoff, Douglas (2003). *Open Source Democracy. How Online Communication is Changing Offline Politics*. London: Demos.

Sen, Amartya (2002). 'The Science of Give and Take', *New Scientist* 174 (2340): 51–2.

Sennett, Richard (1998). *Corrosion of the Character. The Personal Consequences of Work in the New Capitalism*. New York and London: W. W. Norton & Company.

Sennett, Richard (2003). *Respect in the World of Inequality*. New York and London: W. W. Norton & Company.

Sennett, Richard (2006). *The Culture of the New Capitalism*. New Haven and London: Yale University Press.

Seppälä, Juha (2004). *Routavuosi* [Frost Year]. Juva: WSOY.

Shiva, Vandana (2001). *Protect or Plunder? Understanding Intellectual Property Rights.* London: Zed Books.

Shiva, Vandana (2003). 'Globalization and Its Fall Out', http://www. transcend.org/tpu/ (retrieved 26 December 2003).

Stallman, Richard (2002). *Free Software, Free Society. Selected Essays of Richard M. Stallman.* Boston: GNU Press.

Suoranta, Juha (2003) 'The World Divided in Two: Digital Divide, Information and Communication Technologies, and the "Youth Question"', *Journal for Critical Education Policy Studies* 1 (2), http://www.jceps.com/?pageID=article&articleID=16 (retrieved 8 April 2004).

Suoranta, Juha, and Hanna Lehtimäki (2004). *Children in the Information Society. The Case of Finland.* New York: Peter Lang.

Tabb, William (2001). 'Globalization and Education as a Commodit', *Clarion* (Summer). http://www.psc-cuny.org/jcglobalization.htm (retrieved 5 July 2006).

Tammilehto, Olli (2003). 'Globalisation and Dimensions of Povert', http://global.finland.fi/english/publications/pdf/tammilehto_globalisation. pdf (retrieved 1 January 2004).

Tapscott, Don (1998). *Growing up Digital. The Rise of the Net Generation.* New York: McGraw-Hill.

Tarjanne, Pekka (2002). 'The United Nations Information and Communication Technologies Task Force', http://www.connect-world. com/Articles/old_articles/PekkaTarjanne.htm (retrieved 6 March 2007).

Thomson, Iain (2003). 'From the Question Concerning Technology to the Quest for Democratic Technology: Heidegger, Marcuse, Feenberg', in Michael Peter, Mark Olssen and Colin Lankshear (eds), *Futures of Critical Theory. Dreams of Difference.* Lanham: Rowman & Littlefield, pp. 59–72.

Thrift, Nigel (2006). 'Re-inventing Invention: New Tendencies in Capitalist Commodification', *Economy and Society* 35 (2): 279–306.

Toulmin, Stephen (1998). *Kosmopolis. Kuinka uusi aika hukkasi humanismin perinnön* [Cosmopolis. The Hidden Agenda of Modernity]. Porvoo: WSOY.

Tuohinen, P. (2001). 'Netistä toivotaan apua köyhille' [Poor People Put Their Hope in The Net]. *Helsingin Sanomat*, 22 February, C1.

Umbach, Paul, and Matthew Wawrzynski (2005). 'Faculty Do Matter: The Role of College Faculty in Student Learning and Engagement', *Research in Higher Education* 46 (2): 153–84.

Vaidhyanathan, Siva (2004). *The Anarchist in the Library.* New York: Basic Books.

Vail, Jeff (2005). 'Rhizome: Guerrilla Media, Swarming and Asymmetric Politics in the 21st Century', http://www.jeffvail.net/2005/07/rhizome-guerrilla-media-swarming-and.html (retrieved 20 October 2006).

Varto, Juha (1995). 'Ulkopuolisuuden välttämättömyydestä' [The Necessity of Being an Outsider], in J. Suoranta (ed.), *Kuluttaminen ja yksilön kulttuurin kuolema* [Consuming and the Death of Human Culture]. *Lapin yliopiston kasvatustieteellisia julkaisuja* C 11: 53–60.

Vidya Ashram (2008) 'Autonomous Global University', http://www.vidyaashram.org/links.html (retrieved 20 July 2009).

Webster, Frank (2000). *Theories of the Information Society*. New York: Routledge.

Weiner, Eric (2007). 'Readin' Class: Droppin' Out', in Joe Kincheloe and Shirley Steinber (eds), *Cutting Class. Socioeconomic Status and Education*. Boulder: Rowman & Littlefield, pp. 223–64.

Welton, Michael (2002). Listening, Conflict, and Citizenship. Towards a Pedagogy of Civil Society. *International Journal of Lifelong Education* 21 (3), pp. 179–208.

Wheen, Francis (2006). *Das Kapital: A Biography*. London: Atlantic.

Wilkin, Paul (2002). *The Political Economy of Global Communication*. London: Pluto Press.

Williams, Raymond (2005). *Television*. London and New York: Routledge.

Willinsky, John (2006). *The Access Principle*. Cambridge, MA: MIT Press. Also http://mitpress.mit.edu/catalog/item/default.asp?ttype=2&tid=10611.

Willis, Paul (2000). *The Ethnographic Imagination*. Cambridge: Polity Press.

Wired (2003) 'Web Surfers Flock to Al-Jazeera', 1 April, http://www.wired.com/news/politics/0,1283,58313,00.html (retrieved 3 February 2004).

Wittel, Andreas (2001). 'Toward a Network Sociality', *Theory, Culture & Society* 18 (6): 51–76.

WSIS (2003) 'Shaping Information Societies for Human Needs'. Declaration to the World Summit on the Information Society, WSIS Civil Society Plenary, Geneva, 8 December 2003, http://www.itu.int/wsis/docs/geneva/civil-society-declaration.pdf (retrieved 30 December 2003).

Youngman, Frank (1986). *Adult Education and Socialist Pedagogy*. London: Croom Helm.

Youngman, Frank (2000). *The Political Economy of Adult Education and Development*. London and New York: Zed Books.

Žižek, Slavoj (1998). 'A Leftist Plea for Eurocentrism', *Critical Inquiry* 24 (4): 988–1009.

Žižek, Slavoj (1999a). 'Human Rights and its Discontents'. Lecture at the Bard College, 15 November 1999, http://www.lacan.com/zizek-human.htm (retrieved 6 March 2007).

Žižek, Slavoj (1999b). 'You May', *London Review of Books* 21 (6), http://www.lrb.co.uk/v21/n06/zize01_.html (retrieved 11 April, 2004).

Žižek, Slavoj (2001). *On Belief.* Routledge: London.

Žižek, Slavoj (2002a). 'A Plea for Leninist Intolerance', *Critical Inquiry* 28 (Winter): 542–66.

Žižek, Slavoj (2002b). 'A Cyberspace Lenin: Why Not?', *International Socialism Journal* 95, http://pubs.socialistreviewindex.org.uk/isj95/zizek.htm (retrieved 7 October 2006).

Žižek, Slavoj (2004a). *Organs without Bodies. On Deleuze and Consequences.* London: Routledge.

Žižek, Slavoj (2004b). 'The Parallax View', *New Left Review* (January/February).

Žižek, Slavoj (2004c). 'Passion: Regular or Decaf?', http://www.inthesetimes.com/comments.php?id=632_0_4_0_C (retrieved 15 March 2004).

Žižek, Slavoj (2004d). 'Vasemmistolainen vetoomus Eurooppa-keskeisyyden puolesta' [A Leftist Plea for Eurocentrism], *niin & näin* (February).

Žižek, Slavoj (2006a). 'Repeating Lenin', http://www.marxists.org/reference/subject/philosophy/works/ot/zizek1.htm#49 (retrieved 13 October 2006).

Žižek, Slavoj (2006b). 'No One Has To Be Vile', *London Review of Books* 28, http://lrb.co.uk/v28/n07/zize01_.htm (retrieved 4 October 2006).

Žižek, Slavoj (2007a). 'Resistance is Surrender', *London Review of Books*, 15 November. http://www.lrb.co.uk/v29/n22/zize01_.html (retrieved 17 December 2007).

Žižek, Slavoj (2007b). *The Universal Exception.* New York: Continuum.

Žižek, Slavoj (2008). *Violence.* New York: Picador.

INDEX

Compiled by Sue Carlton